You Gave Me Hope (My Story)

You Gave Me Hope (My Story)

An in-depth look at the writing of the songs, the scriptures used, and the sermons written during this project, the life events and the application of God's Word during the ups and downs of real-life that inspired the creation of this book.

Ricky Byrum

Ricky Byrum – You Gave Me Hope (music cd) available at: http://itunes.apple.com/album/id1608761455?ls=1&app=itunes

Copyright © 2022 Ricky Byrum – Burning Bush Productions

All rights reserved. No unauthorized duplication without written consent.

All scripture references are from the King James Bible. Copyright © 1976

Some notes were taken from Human Life International (The Miracle of Fetal Development) by Brian Clowes, Ph.D. (https//www.hil.org/resources/miracle-fetal-development/)

ISBN: 9798810790587 (paperback)

In memory of Betty Jo Savage Umphlett
(Miss you, Mom)

Contents

Preface	ix
Thank You	xi
Introduction	xiii
Chapter 1: You Gave Me Hope	1
Lyrics	3
Scripture	5
Hope Thou in God	7
Life Stories	11
Chapter 2: Keep Your Eyes on Jesus	15
Lyrics	17
Scripture	19
Keep Your Eyes on Jesus	21
Life Stories – Driving to Work One Day	25
Chapter 3: Mindful of Me	27
Lyrics	29
Scripture	31
Mindful of Me	33
Life Stories – I Was Born a Poor Wayfaring Stranger	41
Chapter 4: Love	45
Lyrics	47
Scripture	49

The Cross of Calvary	51
Life Stories – Mr. Presley, Family and Food	61

Chapter 5: Jesus Is Alive   65
    Lyrics   67
    Scripture   69
    I Shall Arise   73
    Life Stories – When I Go to the Hospital,
      I Am Alive in Christ   79

Chapter 6: New Kingdom   83
    Scripture   85
    Sermon – Why Gamble with Your Soul?   89
    Life Stories – On My Way Home   95

Postscript   105

Preface

I want to take this opportunity to thank every participant of both the CD and this book.

It is a gift from God that He allowed me to create this magnificent body of work at this stage of my life. Moses waited 40 years in the desert before being sent back to Egypt to lead the Israelites out. Many ministers have preached that it took God 40 years to get Egypt out of Moses so he could lead God's people out of Egypt. I suppose it took God 40 years to get the world out of me so He could use me too! Amen.

Thank You

(This is not at all inclusive. I appreciate all my people past and present.)

I want to thank my wife Eva and our kids – Briana, Brandon, Luther, and Zachary. I love you with all my heart! Blessings to my beloved sister and her husband, Danny. Much love to my stepdad Jimmy and his kids – Rhonda and Joey (and the extended family and friends) I love you all! All my past and present co-workers). Especially Miss Dora, Leroy Mallette, Chad Jones (the Gatlings), and Wesley Dorsey, who pray with me. Tim Hobbs, Joe Koten, Cort Moore, Patrick Luttig, (Robert Cobb – who encourages me).

My lifelong friends – Larry & Peggy Jernigan (Jernigan family). Kevin & Mitzi Buck, Brian & Sema Panther. Please know how special you are! Thank you to my mighty home church Higher Ground IPHC. And to my beloved Conarista Baptist, who has allowed me to sing and minister for two and half years. Special thanks to Carol Phillips for years of graphic design.

To my precious brother Thomas Arthur, who encouraged me to begin the whole process of recording. It would not have happened without your artistry and engineering prowess. We've come a long way together, my brother. I pray to the Lord, our journey's just begun!

Introduction

This book is about my journey of writing and recording the CD "You Gave Me Hope." But it's more than that. Over the last two and a half years, I've been blessed to write and record these wonderful few songs chosen out of many songs! These were written with sermons inspired by the Holy Spirit of God Almighty. It was the best of times and the worst of times. I was absolutely excited to be writing and recording new material. Yet my mother and sister were ill and hospitalized during a global pandemic! Life was uncertain, and every relationship was strained with isolation and concern. The emotion can be felt in many places, both in sound and words. Thank you for walking with me on my journey. If one person finds Jesus or is encouraged in *Any* way – *It is worth it all!* God bless you and yours.

Ricky Byrum
March 1, 2022

CHAPTER 1
You Gave Me Hope

Lyrics

Ricky Byrum 2022 ©

When I'm in the valley or top of the mountain
I'm never alone, never alone
    Bridge
You wrap your arms around me and warm my soul
You fill me with Your Spirit, Lord, Your love's worth more than gold.
    Chorus
Reached out to me when I was down
You reached way down low and took me out
Reached out to me and made me whole
You dried my eyes and gave me hope (You gave me hope)
    Solo
When I'm in the ocean or wilderness
You give me peace, in You, I rest
    Bridge
You wrap Your arms around me and warm my soul
You fill me with Your Spirit, Lord, Your love's worth more than gold.
    Chorus
Reached out to me when I was down
You reached way down low and took me out
Reached out to me and made me whole
You dried my eyes and gave me hope (You gave me hope) x3

Scripture

Psalm 42:11

Why art thou cast down, O my soul? And why art thou disquieted within me?

Hope thou in God! For I shall yet praise Him, who is the health of my countenance and my God.

Sermon May 9, 2021, Hope Thou In God

Prayer – Heavenly Father, In Thy Magnificent Name, I humbly come as your servant.

And a servant to these – your people. Hide me, O God, behind Your cross. That You may speak through me words of encouragement. For You alone are God. You are in absolute control. (Even when the whole world seems to have gone astray).

You are victorious, King Jesus! You fight for Your children! Come Holy Spirit! To the glory of God the Father, In Jesus Christ Holy Name.

Amen

Sermon Message – Hope Thou In God

We see the writer of the Psalms is King David. He's a man, just like any other human being. He has emotions and strengths and weaknesses just like the rest of us. But as we see in the scriptures, David's always coming back to the center. He's always turning his eyes, his mind, and his heart back to God, which in turn leads his hands and his feet.

In Psalm 42:1-3, As the hart panteth for the water brooks, my soul panteth after Thee O God. My soul thirsteth for God, the living God:

when shall I come and appear before God. My tears have been my meat day and night, while they continually say unto me, where is thy God.

But in verse 4, we see what David does to change his circumstances, and he begins to turn things around. Verse 4 says – When I remember these things, I pour out my soul in me: for I had gone with the multitude, I went with them to the house of God, with the voice of joy and praise, with a multitude that kept Holyday.

Verse 5 says – Why art thy cast down, O my soul? And why art thou disquieted in me? Hope thou in God, for I shall yet praise Him for the help of His countenance.

Hope Thou in God

David's saying no matter what, I'm putting my hope in You, O God! I'm going to give You all my praise! For You alone are worthy! Despite whatever's going on here in this situation or in this world, You are my God and my King! Hallelujah! I know you'll see me through this trial as you've done before! Glory to God, somebody say amen!

David says in verse 6 – O my God, my soul is cast down within me: therefore will I remember thee from the land of Jordan, and of the Hermonites from the hill Mizar.

Psalm 42:7 – Deep calleth to deep at the noise of his waterspouts, all thy waves and thy billows are gone over me. 8 Yet the Lord will command His loving kindness in the daytime, and the night His song shall be with me and my prayer unto the God of my life.

In summary,

1. David's hurting here. He's got some things going on. And it's a test of his faith. Many believe this was when his son Absalom attempted a hostile takeover of his Kingdom. (this is a reminder to us, there are consequences to sin even after God forgives you) Amen
2. David cries out to God. O, GOD! He takes all his feelings and emotions to God in deep prayer, he gets God's attention. More likely, God now has David's attention.
3. He tells God all about it. He doesn't take it to some guy down the road. He gives it all to God. He pours out his soul unto God! Hallelujah! David's known for fasting and prayer.

4. David goes to church! He's not at the bar drowning his sorrows in a drink or a substance or a pill! He's at church!
   CAN'T YOU SEE DAVID AT THE ALTAR RIGHT NOW?
   I can…
5. David asks himself again, assuredly in a different tone, "why are you downcast, O my soul? "Then he tells himself to Hope Thou In God!
6. He remembers what God's done previously. This is huge for us today, brothers and sisters. The enemy of our soul wants to distract you from remembering all that God's done for us. Including today.
7. Deep calleth to deep. If there's a need, there's got to be a God to answer that need.
8. David admits he's struggling. God already knows our hearts and our thoughts.
   In fact, they're recorded. We should do as David did and confess all before God. How much stress and heartache do we bear by holding it all in?
9. He speaks to God about his enemy. So now he brings God into the fight. Many times we're fighting battles we should never be involved in.
   Amen?
10. David encouraged himself. Hope Thou In God. Praise will make you happy even in heartache. In fact, you can have joy continuously even when happiness is gone! Glory to God! David said, "You are my health and my smile." Glory to God!

Hope is the most powerful gift given by God. It's absolutely free!!! Love is the most powerful force there is. Because God is love and created love. Therefore Hope is the greatest gift to a fallen world because of what God did to save us.

The whole world's been given the bible with all kinds of historical evidence and scientific discoveries as a reference to what the bible has stated. Thus confirming people, places, and events that scripture has told us about. All pointing to a divine creator that loved us enough even before He made anything, He planned to take our place on that cross. And the salvation He provides to all who shall believe is genuine HOPE! It's an eternal Hope that God is who He says He is. And any who will confess Jesus is Lord and died for our sins and rose again shall be saved. As well, any who need to rededicate themselves afresh He can do that too! It all happens because the Holy Spirit comes because Jesus is alive! Amen.

In closing – Please stand

So now we must trust in God today. Proverbs 3:5 and 6 – say: Trust in the Lord with all your heart and lean not on your own understanding. In all thy ways, acknowledge Him, and He shall direct your paths. We do this by keeping our eyes on Jesus and not on the cares of this world,

Let us pray – Father, You are our blessed hope! You are our redeemer. And our glorious King. Our God. We seek Your face and Your heart. Above all things, we need You the most! Please forgive us of any known or unknown sin Father God. Bless us, O God, that we will be a blessing to others. That people will see, hear and feel you in us. So that people will be saved, delivered, and filled with Your Holy Spirit. And give them HOPE!

If any need to be saved, say this with me. Jesus, save me. Heal me and deliver me. Fill me with Your Holy Spirit.

To the glory of God the Father, In Jesus Christ Mighty Name,
Amen.

One second in hell's too long.
One second in heaven's worth it all.
I bless you all today, and every family represented.
Romans 15:13 says – Now the God of Hope, fill you with all joy and peace in believing, that ye may abound in hope, through the power of the Holy Ghost. Amen!

Life Stories

Two and a half years ago, my son Zachary and I were attending our normal church service at Higher Ground in Ahoskie, NC. We were at the far right if you were facing the stage/ altar. It was a great service! The house was packed, and the Holy Spirit was moving throughout the church. Ray Faircloth Sr. was preaching up a storm, and Ray Jr. was laying it down musically! We were having a great Sunday service! People came to the altar for prayer at the end. Zach and I would often lay hands on people and say a prayer for them. That's just what ministers do!

This particular Sunday stands out as I had a feeling the whole service that I wanted to be up there preaching and singing myself. More than usual. If you're called to do something, It's in you. Yes, you enjoy attending events where other people do what you're called to do. But ultimately, it's going to come out of you.

So at the close of service, I looked at Zach and said, "you know I want to finish with singing and preaching." Zach said with his infinite wisdom, "well, let's pray on it."

You see, I've been a musician since I was sixteen years old. I've been a Christian since I was eight years old. I was rededicated in 1995. And a Christian recording artist since 2002. I've had music on the radio and in the newspapers with the various bands I was in. The first band I joined was called Apexx with my buddy Thomas Arthur, Henry Wilkins, and Joe Pierce. (who are now active in church, by the way).To be kids, we were very good! All the bands I had the pleasure to be in had the potential to have gone pro. Very talented people. I have to stop to thank a few friends and musicians who I love and who helped me along the way.

(Not at all inclusive): Brian Williams, Rob Blankenship, Rick Thompson, Brian Athur, Myles Brooklyn, David Sadowski, Big Dave. Biker Dave, Troy Anderson, (Filmore Brinkley), who drove the truck). Frank Pierce, Chris Clark, Todd Jenkins, and Jeff Preziotti, who was not only a remarkable drummer, he was one of the men who led me to rededicate my life to Christ with Frank Baldwin and John McSharry. I dedicated my CD – "Time To Rise" to Jeff. I tell his story of unwavering faith while battling terminal cancer annually.

It was not God's plan for my gift to be used for the world. So even as a Christian musician, the business of music was in my blood. Including some of the CDs I recorded for fun and the quality's rough and largely recorded live, I still put them out there. Even though the quality wasn't the same as a million-dollar studio (that I have been blessed to sometimes use), it was my way of expression. The mindset was although I was a Christian, I still had the business side in my spirit. Therefore, God took me to the desert for 40 years to get the world out of me (Egypt) before He'd let me truly get involved in music again.

He let me know that He would largely take music from me to put me into pulpits. This would require me to be into His Word heavily!

And I would be invited to do weddings and funerals for people that wanted a minister they could relate to. And one they knew. Sometimes they were folks that didn't attend a building we would call church. But that doesn't mean they all didn't know God. And who's to say seeds didn't get planted along the way as well? It didn't matter what nationality or who or where. If God was behind it, I showed up! Sometimes way back in the field or in the yard. Or an old shed turned into a church. You might be surprised at the places God will show up if you call on Him. That is exciting to me!

But this Sunday, Zach and I prayed. Within 48 hours, my long-time family friend Jimmy Smith from our old home church of Reynoldson Baptist called. Jimmy was the minister for Conarista Baptist. Jimmy called and said he needed a favor for me to preach for him. So I was able to do that. And before long, he called again and said he needed another favor. He needed me to preach again; however, he was soon retiring, and he had put my name in the hat to help. That was over two and half years ago. I've been preaching and singing there almost every Sunday I'm off.

God is faithful! But I had to die out to myself. I had to die out of the part of it that's about me or putting my own name out there, if you will. God wanted me and my heart first. Then He gave me more of His heart which is about people. He had to get Egypt out of me prior to me leading people out of Egypt.

CHAPTER 2
Keep Your Eyes on Jesus

Lyrics

Ricky Byrum 2022 ©

Imagine a world with no distraction
No image text or ring
Just the call of the Savior
Come unto me
    Bridge
He's calling, calling
    Chorus
Keep your eyes on Jesus
The way the truth the life
Keep your eyes on Jesus
Don't let Him pass you by
Imagine a world with no distraction
No sickness, war, or sin
Just the love of the Father
That never ends
    Bridge
He's calling, calling
    Chorus
Keep your eyes on Jesus
The way the truth the life
Keep Your eyes on Jesus
Don't let Him pass you by x2

Scripture

Hebrews 12:1-2

Therefore, since we are surrounded by so great a cloud of witnesses, let us also lay aside every weight and sin which clings so closely, and let us run with endurance the race which is set before us, Looking Unto Jesus, the founder, and perfecter of our faith, who for the joy that was set before Him endured the cross, despising the shame, and is seated at the right hand of the Throne of God.

Sermon January 22, 2021, Keep Your Eyes on Jesus
Prayer – Lord, I believe You are moving amongst the earth! I believe You are raising David's and Deborah's in this end-time hour. Spiritual warriors that will be led by Your Holy Spirit. Please hide me behind Your cross and speak through me to Your people. That I may give them encouragement to continue this spiritual battle. The victory's been one, and we're marching to get our crown. To which we'll lay it at Your feet!

In Jesus Christ's Mighty Name.
Amen

God's looking for spiritual leaders. To the older folk, I want you to know God's looking for the character and humility of Moses. We see Moses as a spiritual GIANT! God even calls him a friend. He's the man that conquered the most powerful nation at that time with only a stick in his hand!

But little known is that Moses is classified as the most humble man on earth. So he was moldable in the hands of Almighty God. He was obedient. He listened to God and spoke to Him every single day. He was willing to die and even suffer in hell for the souls he was put in charge of. Even when God wanted to destroy them due to their continuous disobedience to God. (after they had seen the miraculous power of God in their deliverance when Moses led them out of Egypt)

That's why God's power flowed in and through Moses. God knew He could trust Moses.

Could it be that we're not seeing the signs and wonders of God in our day because God can't trust us? Maybe we better start Looking unto Jesus our Lord and our God!

Over the last few generations, the church has fallen prey to the enemy. Matthew 6:24 says we can't serve two masters. You can't serve God and mammon. (Money)

The church has fallen to 1. Financial gain. 2. Fear. 3. Traditions of men. 4. Doctrines of devils. 5. Power and popularity.

1 Thessalonians 5:22 says for us to – Abstain from all appearance of evil.

Keep Your Eyes on Jesus

God's shifting and moving things around. The status quo isn't going to work in the days ahead. We'll take part in the Kingdom work of God, or we'll drown in the kingdom of darkness.

Elijah's spirit will come upon our younger people. They will be the David's and Deborah's of this age. They are hungry for the true Spirit of God. Many want to believe in something real! They want to know God's real and He loves them. We, the church as a whole, have failed to deliver to our youth. How do you think God feels about that?

This message of the Kingdom of God was the mandate and precept passed from Adam to you and me. We've created all kinds of religions and creeds and traditions throughout the history of the world! We've made an absolute mess of the Kingdom principles of God.

Myself included. But we don't have time to stay off course. The hour's very late. We must quickly repent to God and take our place in the government of Jesus Christ.

There are only two governments that operate Heaven and earth.

1. The creator of all things is God. His rule is supreme. He rules over everything that exists or will exist.
2. Satan has a temporary lease on the earth as Adam gave it to him in the fall of mankind.

Adam, a son of God, was given dominion and authority over all the affairs on earth. His willful disobedience forfeited his power over to Satan.

Jesus Christ has destroyed Satan's power by His death and resurrection. Glory hallelujah! Somebody say amen!

We see the darkness moving into every aspect of our lives here on earth. The light of the Gospel of Jesus Christ is the ONLY power that can destroy it. And that is our two options.

> Door number 1. is the eternal life and love of Almighty God. And peace here on earth as well.
> Door number 2. is the false promise of Satan, who wishes only to destroy you and everything and everyone in your life. Forever!

God will not share His glory. But He wishes nothing more than to share His love and His power. That's why He sent His Holy Spirit back in Acts 2 at Pentecost. We need the power of God to sustain us in this hour. As God told the Israelites in Egypt – place the BLOOD OF THE LAMB over your doorposts. I'm sending an angel of death throughout the land. And all the homes without it, the first born of man and beast, will die. On Noah's day 8, people got in the ark and were saved. Even more, only Enoch was raptured off the planet before the destruction of the entire earth by water.

How many will be saved in our day?

It all starts by KEEPING OUR EYES ON JESUS, the way, the truth. The life. Amen.

Hebrews 13:8 says – He's the same yesterday, today, and forever.

He walked on water in the past. He had power over nature and over all creation.

Demons feared Him. He had power over life and death. Jesus is God Almighty in the flesh, folks!

I want to see another end-time move of God every bit as strong or stronger than they had in the Azusa Street revivals in 1906-1908. Lord, do it again!

Start right here in me!

If any need me to pray with you for any reason, I'm right here. If you need to be saved, healed, or burdens lifted from you, I'm your brother. And I love you. God loves you!

Let us pray.

Most High God, please don't pass us by today. Come touch us right where we are. Lead us by Your Mighty Spirit today. That we'll be about Your Kingdom Business. Which is saving souls and changing lives. If there's one here today that doesn't know you let them say this prayer with me. Our Father who is in heaven. I believe that Jesus died and rose again for me. Save me, Lord. Fill me with Your Holy Spirit. Come live inside me forever! In Jesus Christ's Name. Amen.

God go with these people today. Protect and provide for them, and every family represented. I bless you all and those you love. In Jesus Mighty Name. Amen.

Life Stories – Driving to Work One Day

⁓

I remember riding down the road going to work about a year or so ago.

It was about 3:30pm, and it was a beautiful day outside. It was the first set of my shift.

Either a Monday after a weekend off or a Friday where I work the whole weekend.

I work 12-hour night shifts. Needless to say, I just wasn't feeling it all.

A lot was going on in my life. In my heart and in my mind. Just like everyone else in the entire world. I was feeling sad and lonely. I was tired! Mentally and physically drained. I just didn't have any gas left in the ole tank. Note: Preachers are people too!

We have the same feelings and trials as everybody else. We've just been called by God to represent Him in the affairs of others here on earth.

So, as I'm driving to work, taking the long scenic way there. (I like it better as it's prettier) I'm listening to preaching and music and attempting to get my soul right before I clock in.

I called my son Zach as I regularly do, to check on him. We inspire one another to stay on the right course you see.

After our initial greetings and conversation, I told him, buddy, "I need a Word."

You must know that Zachary has been given a unique ability to receive from the Holy Spirit a direct Word to encourage me. He does this EVERY SINGLE DAY! (365)

NO JOKE! It's amazing! GLORY HALLELUJAH!

Without hesitating, he said alright. Hebrews 12:2 – Looking Unto Jesus, the founder and perfecter of our faith, who for the joy that was set before Him endured the cross, despising the shame, and is seated at the right hand of the Throne of God.

Instantly the Holy Spirit spoke inside me, telling me to take my eyes off this world and look unto Jesus, the founder, and perfecter of our faith. My faith! My Jesus!

God also instructed me immediately to write a song and a sermon.

That night at work, every spare second I had, The Holy Spirit of God moved my hands across the paper faster than I could write. (my typing is slower)

That night both the song and the sermon, KEEP YOUR EYES ON JESUS, were born.

To God be all the glory and praise! Jesus Christ is Lord and King. Amen.

God bless you!

CHAPTER 3
Mindful of Me

Lyrics

Ricky Byrum 2022 ©

I love to see the flowers bloom
I like to smell the roses
It makes me feel alive
    Bridge – And the world keeps turning
I love to see the leaves change in the fall
I like to see the tractors in the field
It makes me feel alive
    Bridge – And the world keeps turning
    Chorus
When I look into Your heavens, the works of Your hands
The moon and stars You put into place
Who am I, that You are mindful of me
When I hold my wife close and feel the power of love
And stare into my children's face
Who am I, that You are mindful of me
There once stood an old rugged cross
Meant for sinners like me
Where You gave up Your life
    Bridge – So the world would keep turning
    Chorus

Scripture

Psalm 8:3
When I consider Your heavens, the work of Your fingers,
The moon and stars, which You have set in place, what is mankind that You are mindful of them?

Revelation 1:12-19
And I turned to see the voice which spoke with me. And being turned, I saw seven golden candlesticks:
And in the midst of the seven candlesticks one like unto the Son of man, clothed with a garment down to the foot, and the girth about the paps with a golden girdle.
His head and His hairs were like wool, as white as snow, and His eyes were as a flame of fire,
And His feet unto fine brass, as if they burned in a furnace, and His voice as the sound of many waters.
And He had in His right hand seven stars, and out of His mouth went a sharp two-edged sword, and His countenance was as the sun shineth in his strength.
And when I saw Him, I fell at His feet as dead. And He laid His right hand upon me saying unto me, Fear not, I am the first and the last,
I Am He that liveth, and was dead, and behold, I Am alive forevermore. Amen, and have the keys of hell and of death.
Write these things which thou hast seen, and the things which are, and the things which shall be hereafter.

Sermon November 13, 2021, Which Jesus Are You Looking At?
Let us pray.
   My Lord and my God. We have come together to worship You.
   We come to praise Your Name O God! Hide me behind Your cross.
   And may Your Holy Spirit take complete control of this service and of our very lives. In Jesus Christ Majestic Name.
   Amen
   You may be seated.

Mindful of Me

As we celebrate Thanksgiving and Christmas, we often forget the reason for the holidays.

Even more so, the purpose and the PERSON of Thanksgiving and Christmas.

We push aside God's purpose for creating the earth and humanity. We seem to easily forget that He died to redeem us! The whole human race. The same Jesus that created the heavens and the earth by speaking it into existence took our place at the scourging and the cross. Yes, which Jesus are you and I looking at?

Throughout all of human history, we've had encounters with God Himself.

Genesis says after God created the heavens and the earth, He created man in His own image. It says He would walk with them in the cool of the day. I love that scripture! God Almighty walking with His children.

The bible clearly says in Amos 3:7-8 Surely, The Lord God will do nothing, but He revealeth His secret, unto His servants the prophets, The LION hath roared, who will not fear? This is where we lose our proper perspective of God right here. Who will not fear? This is speaking of reverence and respect for God.

God speaks to the hearts and minds of people that are willing to hear. Are we listening?

Except for the 400 years of silence from God between the old and the New Testament, God has always spoken to His people. Imagine the concept of what is being said, The sovereign ruler of the universe wants to speak to you!

Seven hundred years before Jesus, Isaiah said in 6:3

> In the year king, Uzziah died, I saw The Lord sitting on His throne, high and lifted up.
> His train filled the temple. Above it stood the Seraphims: each one had six wings; with twain he covered his face, and with twain, he covered his feet, and with twain, he did fly.
> And one cried to another, and said, Holy, Holy, Holy, is the Lord of hosts: the whole earth is full of His glory! And the posts of the door moved at the voice of Him that cried, and the house was filled with smoke.
> Then said I, woe is me! For I am undone, because I am a man of unclean lips, and I dwell in the midst of a people of unclean lips: for mine eyes have seen the KING, the LORD of HOSTS.

The Apostle John saw the same thing in Revelation 4:8.

> The four beasts had each of them six wings about him, and they were full of eyes within: and they rested not day and night, saying, Holy, Holy, Holy, Lord God Almighty, which was, and is to come.

Hallelujah! This is what two men from two different time periods saw! We need to put ourselves there in our minds right now. For this is the person in charge of Everything! You and I are not in charge. Satan is not in charge; God Almighty's in charge of what's happening in heaven and what's happening on earth.

We need to decide who we're going to follow.

Moses was classified as a friend of God. He sat with God and talked to Him. This is what God says. He desired to see God, and God let him see Him yet from behind, As no one can see God's face and live due to the fallen state of man.

God agreed to let Moses see him, so He put Moses on the cliff of the rock and covered it with His hand as He passed by. Exodus 33:22

God doesn't want to be separated from us. We choose that when Adam sinned. We choose that unto ourselves when we choose sin over the Savior.

So as we approach the holiday season of Jesus' birth, it's only appropriate to contemplate who this man is called Jesus?

Does the perception we have of Jesus match up with who the Bible says He is?

Everywhere we turn this time of year, we see a baby in a manger. We may even see Mary holding her baby boy. And indeed, that may even warm our hearts as we ponder that.

Or we all have seen the Michael Angelo painting of the Lord's supper. Jesus being portrayed as a somber caucasian, European man. We all have images of an empty tomb come Easter.

I suggest we take a closer look at who this man called Jesus actually is.

It's time we get a closer look at the Christ of Christmas.

The apostle Paul tells us in 2 Corinthians 12 – It is not expedient for me doubtless to glory. I will come to visions and revelations of the Lord. I knew a man in Christ above fourteen years ago (whether in the body, I can not tell, or whether out of the body, I can not tell: God knoweth) such a one caught up to the third heaven.

How that he was caught up in paradise and heard unspeakable words, which are not lawful for a man to utter.

Of such a one will I glory: yet of myself I will not glory, but in my infirmities.

Paul is telling us that when he was caught up in heaven, either in a vision or in person, he heard things too great to be spoken on earth.

Bible readers know that Paul has one of the greatest conversion testimonies there is.

Paul, formerly known as Saul, was a highly educated man in Jewish law. He was born and raised as a Pharisee. He was commissioned by the Jewish religious leaders to hunt, persecute, imprison and even murder the Christians. They wanted to stop the early followers of Christ at all costs!

That is until Paul had a physical encounter with the risen Jesus who appeared unto him on the road to Damascus. Christ chose to appear unto him in the same pillar of fire that led the Israelites by night out of Egypt. Aa well the cloud by day.

> Acts 9:39
> Suddenly, there shone round about him a light from heaven, and he fell to the earth. And he heard a voice from heaven saying, "Saul, Saul, why persecutest thou me?"
> And Paul said, "who art thou Lord?" And the Lord said, "I AM Jesus whom thou persecutest. It is hard to kick against the pricks."

I implore you that it was indeed the same Pillar of fire back in Exodus that engaged Paul on that Damascus road. Hebrews 13:8 says, I AM the same yesterday, today, and forever! Glory hallelujah! I feel the Holy Ghost up in here! Somebody say amen!!!!

WE SERVE AN INCREDIBLE, INDESCRIBABLE, ALL-POWERFUL GOD! Far too big to imagine or describe! When we, the saved believers of Jesus, see Him face to face, it will be the most wonderful, shocking moment in our lives forever! For the unbeliever, it will be the most fearful, heartbreaking moment they'll ever face. As they realize a stark reality of the most precious gift of eternal life has been spurned and wasted! Forever!!!

That my brothers and sisters must motivate us to the soul to:

1. Remain absolutely rooted and grounded in God and His Word.
2. To be extremely activated in winning souls unto the Lord!

Anyone with eyes and ears and a beating heart can know that time is hurling towards a climax! Amen???

In a nursing home ministry one time, I told the elderly or feeble that no one's forgotten by God! Your availability of time towards prayer is as or more powerful in the Kingdom building of God than any mega ministry on planet earth!

God created everything that is by merely speaking. The same

person that spoke things too massive and vast to comprehend, millions and millions of light-years away, could indeed say, "Be no more." And EVERYTHING would DISAPPEAR as if it never existed.

Think about that for a minute. Let that sink in...

Remember this holiday season. Remember that every day you wake up and have the breath of life in you! Remember that your body's able to get out of bed and walk. Think about that as you kneel down to pray in the best of times. Or the worst of times! He's God Almighty!

Luke 1:37 says NOTHING'S IMPOSSIBLE FOR GOD!

2 Timothy 4:8 says, God is a righteous judge. Everyone born will be judged by the only one worthy. The Lord Jesus Christ. The creator and sustainer of all things.

Note: the number one cause of death in all the world, including in America, is the ending of the life of babies in the womb. God's not happy about that. 1 John 4 says God is love.

God loves everyone equally. Children are very dear to God the Father.

Matthew 19:14 But Jesus said, Suffer the little children, and forbid them not, to come unto me: for such is the Kingdom of Heaven.

As well, how we treat women and the elderly or those with special needs is of utmost importance to God. All of life is extremely special to God the Father. The model prayer says – THY KINGDOM COME, THY WILL BE DONE, IN EARTH AS IT IS IN HEAVEN.

Are we managing life on earth as it is in heaven? We're supposed to! Let's look at some scientific facts about the wonders of fetal development.

Some of the notes are taken from Human Life International (The Miracle of Fetal Development) by Brian Clowes, Ph.D. (https//www.hil.org/resources/miracle-fetal-development/)

Note: To have a conception, one million sperm cells are released amongst one million egg cells. The right sperm out of a million must find the right one out of a million egg cells to begin the fertilization process. Amazing!

On the first day, the first of four cell divisions take place as the fertilized ovum travels down the mother's Fallopian tubes towards the uterus, all the while being nourished and protected by the mother's body.

After 5-9 days, it implants in the uterus and, from this point onward to about eight weeks, is known as an embryo.

At 3 weeks, the preborn child's heart is in an advanced stage of formation. The child's eyes begin to form, and their brain, spinal column, and nervous system are virtually complete.

At 4 weeks, the child's muscles are developing. Their arm and leg buds are visible, and the first neocortical cells appear. The neocortex is the seat of complex thinking and reasoning, a feature in no other mammal. The embryo has grown in size by a factor of 10,000 since fertilization and is now about 6-7 millimeters long. About a quarter of an inch.

At 5 weeks, the pituitary gland is forming. Often called the master gland since it controls most of the endocrine glands. Additionally, the baby's mouth, ears, and nose are taking shape.

At 6 weeks, the baby's heart energy output is an incredible 20% of that of an adult. The cartilage skeleton is completely formed, and bone formation begins.

At 43 days, the baby's brain waves can be recorded.

At 45 days, the baby begins spontaneous and voluntary body movements, and their milk teeth buds are present.

At 7 weeks, the baby's lips are sensitive to touch, and their ears resemble their family's. The first fully developed neurons (nerve cells) appear on the top of the spinal cord, beginning the construction of the brain stem, which regulates vital functions such as breathing, the heartbeat, and blood pressure.

At 8 weeks, the preborn baby is well-proportioned, about one and a half inches long. All organs are present, complete, and functioning except the lungs.

At 9 weeks, the preborn child will bend his fingers around an object placed in their palm. The child's fingernails are forming, and the child sucks their thumb.

At 10 weeks, all sections of the body are sensitive to touch. The baby swallows, squints, and frowns.

At the end of the first trimester, 12 weeks, vigorous activity shows the baby's distinct personality. Sleep patterns differ. The baby can kick, hiccup, and turn and open its mouth.

At 13 weeks, the preborn child's facial expressions resemble those of their parents. The child's vocal cords and external sex organs are present.

At 4 months, the preborn baby can grasp their hands, turn somersaults, and swim. The child's mother may feel the baby's movements for the first time.

At 7 months, the baby weighs about 2.2 lbs. The baby's lungs are capable of breathing air. The baby's eye teeth are present. The baby's hands can support their entire weight at this time. Of the 45 total generations of cell development that will take place by mature adulthood, 38 have already taken place. The baby now has about 300 billion cells.

Moving forward, on the baby's birthday, the baby releases hormones that trigger labor. The baby now has about 2,000,000,000,000 cells.

Jeremiah 1:5
Before I formed thee in the belly, I knew thee, and before thou camest forth out of the womb, I sanctified thee, and I ordained thee a prophet unto the nations.

When Mary held and kissed her little baby, she was holding the creator of the heavens and the earth. I understand that's too much to grasp. But by the mercy and revelation of God, we got to hold onto that belief.

You may be asking why I said all this.

I was adopted at 9 months old by a couple who couldn't have a baby.

They chose me because I was the most needy child in the facility.

The only person I knew was my overworked nurse. When she presented me to my potential parents, I clung to her and cried in desperation and fear.

But O, my brothers, and sisters, It was God working out my steps before me.

My life was ordained and orchestrated by the hands that formed me in my biological mother's womb. And I was raised by another mother. Who would go on to work three jobs to care for my sister Vicki and me as she was alone raising 2 kids. (That's a whole other story)

In closing, as we go our way this holiday season, and see all the lights and the frills, remember the descriptions of Jesus given in the bible.

Remember the baby that was born to take our place. He took on EVERY sin that would ever happen over the course of all time! Every single sin ever committed by humans.

I want you to imagine and envision what Jesus looks like right now. And what He's doing.

He's interceding for you and me against a devil who accuses us day and night.

What Jesus are you and I looking at right now?

More importantly, are we looking for Jesus right now? We don't know the day or hour our time is up. WE MOST CERTAINLY SEE THE HOUR APPROACHING OF HIS CALLING THE CHURCH HOME!

I'm here today as your brother. I love you all. I'm here to pray for you in any need you may have. If you need to come to salvation, or to rededicate your life unto Christ. Or if you have a different kind of need, I'm here.

Let us pray.

Heavenly Father, yes, we celebrate Christmas. When You came to earth as a small child to bear the weight of sin for the whole world. We celebrate that you rose from the dead, defeating death, hell, and the grave! Glory hallelujah! Lord, we celebrate who Your Word says You were, who You are, and who You always will be. Lord of Lords and King of Kings! If there is one today that doesn't know You as a Savior, say this with me – Jesus save. Heal me. Fill me with Your Holy Spirit and make me a new person. In the mighty Name of Jesus Christ! Amen! Praise God!

Now go with the people today Father. I bless them and ask that you protect them and their mind, body, soul, and spirit. Protect their families, especially if traveling. Keep us in Your constant care and provision. To the glory of the Father and empowered by the Holy Ghost! IN JESUS MAGNIFICENT NAME, AMEN

Life Stories – I Was Born a Poor Wayfaring Stranger

I remember the day my dad called me into the bathroom while he was shaving.

He was a truck driver for most of my early years, so we only saw him on weekends.

I suppose I was maybe 7 or 8 years old at the time.

I could tell by the way he called me that this was going to be a serious conversation.

The kind of tone that made you check yourself! Did I do something wrong?

This man was 5 ft. 7, 235 lbs. And he could knock a horse down on its knees with one punch. I witnessed this on a few occasions, as we had 13 horses at one time.

Well, he began the talk while he continued to shave. In fact, he never looked at me.

He said, "you know your mom, and I love you very much." I said yes, sir. I love you too. He began to tell me that I was adopted at about 9 months old. But that didn't change the fact that I was their son. And that they loved me just as much as if they had given birth to me.

This was a critical moment in my life. It did not surprise me or even take me off guard.

I believe I already knew it and was prepared for it.

You see, I have felt like a stranger walking this planet my whole life.

Remembering this moment helped me endure some of the *really* bad times that came in my teenage years. (where our home became a battle zone gripped in fear, anger, tension, and confusion). This was a really strange place where people weren't who you thought they were when you're trying to understand who you are!

I must interject a comment right here. I confessed to Jesus Christ as my Lord and Savior around eight years old or so while watching Billy Graham on TV.

And I knew what I was doing, and I meant it! How I wish I had never allowed myself to waiver in my teenage years. Thankfully, I was able to make that statement in pulpits around my surrounding communities.

I believe God has prepared me to walk this earth with heaven on my mind and in my heart.

The old hymn Poor Wayfaring Stranger (Roud 3339) says, I am a poor wayfaring stranger, while traveling this world below.

There's no sickness, toil, nor danger in that bright land to which I go.

I'm going there to see my mother, my heavenly Father, maybe my adopted dad. And so many others who have gone on before me.

I was born to preach and sing and be a brother to folks. I had two older men who were dear family friends. (Murray Parker and Richard Jernigan) They told me when I was in my 30s that I was to be a preacher. I laughed and told them they had lost their mind! Now, I know they had a connection to God and saw things I couldn't at the time.

Like King David, I am a passionate man. In everything I do!

That comes through in whatever I apply myself to. And I have an incredible sense to protect whoever's in my tribe. Which is always growing as I age and expand out into the world. That's always been in me since I was a little boy. I'd fight a bully quickly! lol

With my wife, my children, and my friends, I especially feel this way.

Even with my church family and co-workers, I have an innate sense of love and compassion for them. I don't like being aggressive. Because I know me. I love deeply. I fight hard. I work hard. I spend a lot of time alone with God reading and praying and writing sermons and music. And I like that. It's who I am. But I love my family and my people greatly! I appreciate them; they try to work with me on all this. (It's hard, I know)

God has given me the ability to feel what others feel. IT'S A HEAVY BURDEN!

But God uses it to show Himself to others. Jesus often went off to Himself to pray.

So being someone who spends a lot of time alone was really God pulling me to Himself so He could mold me into the man He designed me to be.

It took me 40 years to comply with the plan and be tried in the fire to get all the bad stuff out.

Romans 8:28 reminds us that all things work together for good to them that love God, to them who are called according to His purpose.

So, remember that God's greater and bigger than we could ever imagine. His feelings are so much deeper and stronger than we perceive. Sometimes, He allows me a small piece of what He's feeling. It's way too much to absorb! It's so overwhelming!

Psalm 8:3-4
When I consider Thy heavens, the work of Thy fingers, the moon, and stars, which thou hast ordained, What is man, that Thou art mindful of him?

God loves you, my friend. No matter who you are, where you are, or what you have done. Draw closer to God, and He will come closer to you! James 4:8. I know this is true!

I ran from Him for years. I'm so glad I ran back to Him. I trust you will too! No matter how close you are to Him right now, there's always more of Him to receive! Just open your heart more! Trust Him more! Just give Him a chance.

He is the greatest love story ever told! I bless you in Jesus's name! Peace.

CHAPTER 4

Love

Lyrics

Ricky Byrum 2022 ©

Hear me when I call
God of righteousness
You have relieved me in my distress
In my distress
    Bridge
Have mercy on me and hear my prayer
    Repeat
    Chorus
Love breaks the chain
It tears down the wall
Love heals the hurt
Love saves us all
I will praise You
With my whole heart
I will tell of Your works
How you made the stars
    Bridge
Have mercy on me and heal my prayer
    Repeat
    Chorus
Love breaks the chain
It tears down the wall

Love heals the hurt
Love saves us all
    Chorus (soft)
    Chorus

Scripture

~~~~~

Psalm 4

Hear me when I call, O God of my righteousness, Thou hast enlarged me when I was in distress, have mercy on me, and hear my prayer.

Psalm 51

Have mercy upon me. O God, according to Thy loving kindness: according unto the multitude of Thy tender mercies blot out my transgressions.

John 3:16-18

For God so loved the world, that He gave His only Son, that whosoever, believeth in Him should not perish, but have everlasting life. For God sent not His son into the world to condemn the world, but through Him might be saved.

1 John 4:8

He that loveth not, knoweth not God, for God is love.

Sermon (originally written) August 8, 2017, The Cross of Calvary
Preached on a few occasions.
Let us pray.

Heavenly Father, I stand before you most humbly. I seek Your help and guidance in speaking to these people. Your people. We all need more of You. And less of us.

Hide me behind Your cross. Let them see you, hear You, and feel Your presence as we call on Your Holy Spirit to take control of the service. In Jesus' Holy Name. Amen.

You may be seated.

Most people have heard John 3:16 as we read it today. But do we really understand the magnitude of what really happened?

Rome had the people of Israel under their dominant rule and authority. The Jews still had their scriptures from Moses and the law. And they were allowed to worship in the temple.

The Cross of Calvary

However, the Jews were not only under Roman/gentile authority; they were severely taxed by their own theological leaders in the Pharisees and Sadducees. Needless to say, they were anxious for a leader to free them from tyranny. They longed for the Messiah.

But most people didn't even realize that the GREAT I AM of the burning bush was indeed the same GOD in JESUS the CHRIST!

John 3:14 says – And as Moses lifted up the serpent in the wilderness, even so, must the Son of man be lifted up.

> John 3:17–18
> For God sent not His Son into the world to condemn the world, but that the world through Him might be saved.
>
> He that believeth on Him is not condemned: but he that believeth not is condemned already because he hath not believed in the name of the only begotten Son of God.
>
> (Jesus) who is Lord of Lords and King of Kings.

In 1 John, we get a snapshot of who Jesus is and what He's going to do by going to Calvary and dying on the cross. Jesus, being God in a bodily form, created everything in the universe. So He planned to create people in His own image. And He knew Adam and Eve would fall to Satan's temptation. Thus, bringing everyone else born into a fallen human race. He planned His own death before He made anything!

Revelation 13:8
And all that dwell upon the earth shall worship Him, whose names are written in the Book of Life of the Lamb, slain from the foundation of the world. Amen.

Prior to His coming, He sent prophets that proclaimed a coming Messiah throughout the Old Testament.

Isaiah 7:14, 9-6, Micah 5:2, Zechariah 9:9, Psalm 22:16-18.
In fact, there are at least 55 Old Testament scriptural references to the coming Messiah.
Jesus the Christ.

We see Jesus had a forerunner that paved the way in His cousin John the Baptist.

Matthew 3
In those days came John the Baptist, preaching in the wilderness of Judea, Saying, Repent for the Kingdom of God is at hand.

For this is he that was spoken of by the prophet Esaias, saying, The voice of one crying in the wilderness, Prepare ye the way of the Lord, make his paths straight.

John 1
In the beginning was the Word, and the Word was with God, and the Word was God. The Same was in the beginning with God. All things were made by Him, and without Him was not anything made. In Him was life, and life was the light of men. And the light shineth in darkness, and the darkness comprehended it not.

There was a man sent from God, whose name was John. The same came for a witness, to bear witness of the Light, that all men through him might believe. He was not the Light but was sent to bear witness of that Light. That was true Light, which lighteth every man that cometh into the world. He was in the world, and the world was made by Him, and the world knew Him not. He came unto His own, and His own received Him not.

But as many received Him, to them, he gave the power to become the sons of God, even to them that believe in His name.

Which were born, not of blood, nor of the will of the flesh, nor of the will of man, but of God.

And the Word was made flesh and dwelt among us, and we beheld His glory, the glory as of the only begotten of the Father, full of grace and truth.

John bare witness of Him and cried, saying, This was He of whom I spake, He that cometh after me is preferred before me: for He was before me. And of His fullness have we all received, and grace for grace.

For the law was given by Moses, but grace and truth came by Jesus Christ.

No man hath seen God at any time, the only begotten Son, which is in the bosom of the Father, He hath declared Him.

And this is the record of John when the Jews sent priests and Levites from Jerusalem to ask him, Who art thou?

And he confessed, and denied not, but confessed, I am not the Christ.

And they said unto him, What then? Art thou Elias? And he saith, I am not. Art thou that prophet? And he answered, No.

Then said they unto him, Who art thou? That we may give an answer to them that sent us. What sayest thou of thyself?

He said, I am the voice of one crying in the wilderness; make straight the way of the Lord, as said by the prophet Esaias.

And they were sent by the Pharisees.

And they asked him, and said unto him, Why baptizest thou then if thou be not on Christ, nor Elias, neither that prophet?

John answered them, saying, I baptize with water: but there standeth one among you, whom ye know not,

It is He, who coming after me is preferred before me, whose shoe's latchet I am not worthy to unloose.

These things were done in Bethabara beyond Jordan, where John was baptizing. The next day John seeth Jesus coming unto him, and saith,

Behold the Lamb of God, which taketh away the sin of the world. This is He of whom I said After me cometh a man which is preferred before me: for He was before me.

And I knew Him not: but that He should be made manifest to Israel; therefore I come baptizing with water. And John bare record, saying, I saw a Spirit descending from heaven like a dove, and it abode upon Him.

And I knew Him not: but He that sent me to baptize with water, the same he said unto me, upon whom thou shalt see the Spirit descending, and remaining on Him, the same is He.

Which baptizeth with the Holy Ghost.

Folks, I know that's a lot of reading. But what was said right here is some of the most important, powerful statements ever made!

Notice: We have to take a closer look to see who Jesus actually is to get a better perspective of the importance of Him dying on the cross. If we merely consider Him just a great person who was martyred, WE COMPLETELY MISS THE MOST IMPORTANT MOMENT IN HUMAN HISTORY! WHEN JESUS DIED ON THE CROSS – AND YET ROSE AGAIN ON THE THIRD DAY!

That was GOD, (Emanuel) God with us, taking our place! Absorbing all our sins. Paying the ultimate price so He wouldn't lose us… I hope you're getting this today. For I, too, am a voice crying out in this modern wilderness. Don't miss this! THIS IS YOUR DAY OF SALVATION!

Revelation 13:8
And all that dwell upon the earth shall worship Him, whose names ARE NOT written in the Book of Life of the Lamb, slain from the foundations of the world.

No matter who you are and what you do or don't believe, there will come a day when every single person sees Him; WE ALL WILL FALL DOWN AND WORSHIP! He is God! And there is no other!

> John 4:24
> God is a Spirit: and they that worship Him must worship Him in spirit and in truth.

Jesus is the LOGOS part of the Godhead. There's one, Only one God.

But He works in three aspects. (Or offices)

1. God the Father.
2. God the Son.
3. God the Holy Spirit.

God has these three attributes. Just as I'm a father, son, and husband. Yet, I'm one person. God is all-knowing, all-powerful. And He can be everywhere at once! That's truly amazing! It's far too much to fully understand and comprehend. But deep in the heart of the believer, in our spirit, we believe. Our spirit longs for His Spirit. And to return to Him. That's why it's so important we receive in full, His Holy Spirit. Just as Paul said to John's converts. Have ye received the Holy Spirit since ye believed? They said they had not even heard of the Holy Ghost. And when he baptized them in Jesus's name, they received the Holy Spirit of God. Acts 2:38. Amen!

This is spiritual warfare we're fighting. The enemy of our soul never sleeps! WE CAN'T FIGHT THIS HIM IN OUR OWN STRENGTH OR ABILITY! However, the God in us is far greater than any force that exists!

> 1 John 4:4
> Greater is He that's within me than he that's in the world! Glory hallelujah!

Logos – noun
The Word of God, or principle of divine reason and creative order, identified in the Gospel of John with the second person of the Trinity incarnate in Jesus Christ.

Some notes derived from – Omnipresent God, on the page (All About God).
Omnipotent God – What is Omnipotence?

We have an omnipotent God. He has the ability and power to and over anything. This power is exercised effortlessly. A good example of God's omnipotence is in the name El Shaddai, which means self-sufficient or almighty. God's power is unlimited!

What is Omniscience? It is defined as the state of having total knowledge, the quality of knowing everything. For God to be Sovereign over His creation of all things, whether visible or invisible, He has to be all-knowing. His omniscience is not restricted to any one person in the Godhead – Father, Son, and Holy Spirit are all by nature omniscient.

God is omnipresent (everywhere at once) – How does this impact me?

Throughout the Bible, we see that God is Omnipresent, and it impacts us on a deep level. Psalm 139:7-10 tells us, "Where can I go from Your Spirit? Where can I flee from Your presence? If I go up to the heavens, You are there; if I make my bed in the depths, You are there. I rise on the wings of the dawn. If I settle on the far side of the sea, even there, Your hand will guide me, Your hand will hold me fast."

Matthew 6:6 says, "But when you pray, go to your room, close the door and pray to your Father, who is unseen. Then you, Father, who sees what is done in secret, will reward you."

What do you think about all this? We all have sinned and deserved God's judgment. God, the Father, sent His only Son to satisfy that judgment for those who believe in Him. Jesus, the creator and eternal Son of God, who lived a sinless life, loves us so much that He died for our sins! Taking the punishment that we deserve, was buried and rose from the dead according to the Bible. If you truly believe and trust this in your heart, receiving

Jesus alone as your Savior, declaring, Jesus is Lord, you will be saved, (spared) from judgment and spend eternity with God in heaven.

Now, what is your response to this message? What is your response to Jesus?

If I give you a key that unlocks a particular door to my house, and it's storming terribly outside. Yet if you refuse to go that way, you will not get out of the storm. Nor get in my house at all as you simply want to go your own way.

IT'S STORMING OUTSIDE, DEAR PEOPLE! Jesus has given us all His key to the front door of His house! And like a good Father, He's calling us to come in out of the storm.

It all starts with worship. Just open your heart and worship the Lord. Let go of the cares of this world and tell the Lord Jesus thank you! You and I don't have it all together right now. Don't worry about that now.

Luke 4:8
Jesus answered, "It is written: worship the Lord your God." Hallelujah!!!
Jesus replied," The Scriptures say, You must worship the Lord your God and serve only
Him. It is written."

Exodus 20:3
Thou shalt have no other gods before me. Thou shalt not make unto thee any graven image or any likeness of anything that is heaven above, or that is in the earth beneath, or that is in the water under the earth.

Thou shalt not bow down thyself to them, nor serve them: for I the Lord thy God am a jealous God, visiting the iniquity of the fathers upon the children unto the third and fourth generation of them that hate Me.

In Isaiah 44:6, the Jehovah of the Old Testament identified Himself to Israel with these words:

"Thus saith the Lord the King of Israel, and His redeemer the Lord of hosts: I AM, the first, and I AM the last., besides ME, there is no other god."

In Revelation 1:8-11 the Jesus of the New Testament identified Himself with these words:

> *"I AM ALPHA AND OMEGA, the beginning and the ending, saith the Lord, which is, which was, and which is to come, the Almighty.... The First and the Last."*

We've been distracted and lulled to sleep while our adversary and his cohorts are running wild, destroying everything and everyone he can! America and the rest of the entire world have made idols out of everything!

The historian Will Durant said, "Christianity did not destroy paganism, it adopted it."

As far back in history, all the way to Babylon with Nimrod, and later in Rome, the false precept of a pagan trinity.

They created the worship of false gods in groups of threes.

Rome would later adopt these pagan rituals to include the Christian followers into the governing system. Especially after the Nicean Council meeting 325 AD.

So as we see, we must be aware, that even in our church, our culture, and our community, we're in a spiritual battle for the human soul.

We serve a wonderful, loving Father. Who put His entire essence into a human cell in Mary. Born to die for His children who lost their way. Then He gave His children His very own Spirit that was disconnected by the fall of Adam.

Yes, He is a Father. Yes, He came in a bodily form as the Son. And certainly, His Spirit is Holy as He is Holy. But He is one God.

Exodus 20 says – I AM the Lord your God, and you shall have no other. (singular) One.

In closing, let us stand.

What must one do to be saved? You simply ask Jesus to forgive you of your sins.

Say this with me – Jesus save me. And mean it with all your heart. Jesus, save me. Fill me with Your Holy Spirit. I give You all of me. As You gave me all of You!

I believe You died for me so that I could be saved. Today is my day of salvation! GLORY HALLELUJAH! Jesus is KING! If you've said this and truly meant it, you are now saved and a member of the family and Kingdom of God Almighty! A child and heir of God. Amen!

Romans 10:9 states – Because if thou shalt confess with thy mouth Jesus as Lord, and shalt believe in thy heart that God raised Him from the dead, thou shalt be saved!

Acts 2:38 says – Peter replied, "Repent and be baptized, every one of you, in the name of Jesus Christ for the remission of sins, and ye shall receive the gift of the Holy Spirit.

I encourage you to be baptized and receive power from Heaven to continue in this life in the power and instruction of God. You are saved. This is an outward expression of what's happened on the inside, like a wedding band.

Seek Him daily! He loves you more than you could ever imagine! And so do I. You will never regret being saved, for it lasts an eternity! Amen.

Let's pray – Lord Jesus, Our Most High God, we ask forgiveness for any and all sin. Known and unknown. We don't want anything hindering our prayers or our walk with You. We surrender ourselves completely to You. As we leave this place today, I bless these people and all who they love. Guide us, O God! Protect us. Give us power from the Holy Spirit and the Blood You shed on the Old Rugged Cross of Calvary. Give us hope and protection from Your Mighty angels. Every day! We ask this in the Mighty Name of Jesus! Amen and Amen.

Life Stories – Mr. Presley, Family and Food

In being obedient to God in writing this book, the Lord has spoken to me many, many things. Various memories that span the course of my entire life. This little book doesn't even scratch the surface at all! I can't tell you the number of times people have suggested that I write a book. And yeah, I've certainly considered it. But soon passed it off as not the right time. And it wasn't the right time with God. If the Lord tarries, maybe He'll see fit to continue with this process. Having a body of music and the lyrics, the scriptures, and the sermons together. Closed out by the life stories He's allowed me to live out.

What a novel concept! Only God would answer a prayer that BIG! And in this way.

I can't have a chapter entitled LOVE and not include Mr. Presley. Mr. P., As we affectionately called him, was our pastor at Reynoldson Baptist church.

Mr. P was, at one time, the longest-standing preacher in NC. At that time, he had been preaching for around 35 years. We all loved him immensely! He reminded us all of Abraham Lincoln in his stature and his demeanor. He has since gone on to be with the Lord. And receive an incredible reward, I'm sure!

I remember going to church every Sunday. First, we had Sunday school class then preaching. As an active little boy and then a pre-teen, we didn't grasp the golden nuggets that were being implanted inside us.

Yes, the seeds would lie dormant for a spell. However, in due time they'd bloom and blossom into a beautiful flowering tree of faith!

Glory hallelujah! Somebody say amen!

Mr. P. was from Mississippi. He fit right in with the local town folk. He enjoyed coon hunting and umpiring at the baseball games. He became known as Gates County's preacher. After he officially retired, he expanded that role to the region's preacher.

He filled in everywhere! No one was born, married, or passed away where he wasn't present and involved, And any other life event that occurred along the way.

Note: I have way too much to say about Mr. P. to state it all here. That is a book in itself that should be written. He taught us how to live a life as men of God. Much of my whole neighborhood was dotted with men & women of faith and astounding moral character. Murray Parker, Maryland and Carlton Harrell, Richard Jernigan. All our folks were hard-working people. Lonnie and Mama Carolyn Jernigan allowed me and his four boys to eat him out of the house and home EVERY DAY! My grandfather and uncle were all hard-working men. RL Savage Sr. and Jr. Mr. P. was a blessing and friend to us all! And I believe that Mr. P. saw all of us unto salvation and or rededication to the Lord Jesus Christ. Note to Miss Mary Lee and Florence Harrell, Diane Jernigan, and Aunt Jean. (The Parkers), our block-

Thank you for making our community a great place to live! I love you!

My journey with Mr. P. had a profound change in 1997 when I moved back to Gates County. He took me under his wing as a protege. I would go on to work and teach each and every class from preschool, teens, adults and the elderly men's class. Mr. P. would take me to join him in participating with various revivals in the area. Remember, all my years in music, I was a bassist and a songwriter. Now, I'm up there nervous and playing and singing guitar. I had never been given to stage fright when playing for the world. But, oh my goodness, now it was completely different! I'm standing in God's pulpit number 1. Number 2. I was not a singer or guitarist at all then. (I just fling it out there now) lol

Number 3. I'm up here with one of the finest men that's ever walked the earth!

God and Mr. P had mercy on me. Even through all life's changes and challenges, God had mercy on me and my family. As He does each of us. That is love. Lived out and wonderfully expressed in a man.

I always say that Mr. P. laid the foundation of what would be my ministry. That is found in one of the most beautiful, yet least truly comprehended verses in the Bible.

John 3:16
For God so loved the world. (The whole world), That HE gave His only begotten Son, that (any) should believe in Him, will have everlasting life.

Mr. P. laid that whole foundation of LOVE.

Ray Faircloth Sr. would later help lay the foundation of Holy Spirit POWER! And God Himself is taking it to His climax in THE KINGDOM of God!

That's a very beautiful truth! I'm so THANKFUL! And only God could take a wretch like me, and do something to allow me to love and encourage others in any way. Much less in His Ministry. That's the AMAZING GRACE AND LOVE OF GOD for a sinner like me! Glory hallelujah!

Family

Now, when speaking of family, this includes all the folks past, present and future. Way too many folk to name in this little book. Friends are family by the way. You may be one of the strange folk over there, but you're still family.

Now all the women in my family can absolutely cook like you wouldn't believe! IT'S A WONDER I DON'T WEIGH A LITERAL TON! I'm not joking! Some of the men can cook amazingly well too! Larry Jernigan and Brian Panther, my wife Eva's brother Ron also!

All our family events center around food every time! We can eat around here, folks!

It's a universal language of LOVE. Most of my fondest memories center around the table.

My grandma Byrum parted the RED-SEA one Sunday when we were getting together for a meal. And her daughters, who were cooking, kept asking her questions as she was rocking in her rocker with me at her feet. She quietly stood up, pulled her walker to her and proceeded to the stove, and prepared a feast for a massive amount of people!

Astounding!!!

I saw it in my mom. I saw this in mamma Carolyn. Grandma Sally, for sure. My sister Vicki can cook too! I see it in my wife Eva, who's prepared meals for all six of us for years! Let us never take this supreme act of love and service for granted. Eva and Vicki and our friend's wives are collecting recipes from our loved ones who have now passed on. They're not only keeping a favorite food for us. But they're keeping loving memories that will be passed down for generations. Why? These women have love inside for us. And this is one of many ways they express it. I'm so very proud of them! I know I don't communicate that nearly enough!

This is very Christ-like. The Lord's first miracle was at a wedding feast. John 2 Jesus fed tens of thousands. Matthew 14 and again Matthew 15.

The Lord's supper was an intimate meal with his chosen people before His crucifixion. Matthew 26.

Jesus was found cooking fish on the beach after He arose from the dead. John 21

Lastly, Revelation 19.

The Great God who reigns supreme will speak with a voice like many waters.

Let us be glad and rejoice and give Him honor. For the Marriage of the Lamb is come, and His wife hath made herself ready! And he saith unto me, write, Blessed are they which are called unto the Marriage Supper of the Lamb. And he saith unto me, These are true sayings of God. Amen.

There's nothing like LOVE. It is of and from God. 1 John 4:16 God is Love. And if we don't love one another, the Love of God's not in us.

CHAPTER 5
Jesus Is Alive

Lyrics

Ricky Byrum 2022 ©

I want Holy fire
Devil, you're a liar
By Father in heaven
Jesus is alive,
Jesus is alive
    Chorus
Holy Spirit welcome
You're my desire
Set us on fire
Cuz, Jesus is alive
Because Jesus is alive
Blessed Savior,
Pour out Your Spirit
And wash our cares away
And wash our cares away
    Chorus
Holy Spirit welcome
You're my desire
Set us on fire
Cuz, Jesus is alive
Because Jesus is – alive

Scripture

❦

Please stand for the reading of God's Word.

Micah 7:7-8

Therefore I will look unto the Lord; I will wait for the God of my salvation: my God will hear me. Rejoice not against me, O mine enemy: when I fall, I shall arise, when I sit in darkness, the Lord shall be a light unto me. W

Matthew 28: 1-8

1 At the end of the sabbath, as it began to dawn toward the first day of the week, came Mary Magdalene and the other Mary to see the sepulcher.

2 And, behold, there was a great earthquake: for the angel of the Lord descended from heaven, and came and rolled back the stone from the door, and sat upon it.

3 His countenance was like lightning, and his raiment white as snow:

4 And for fear of him, the keepers did shake and became as dead men.

5 And the angel answered and said unto the women, Fear not ye: for I know that ye seek Jesus, which was crucified.

6 He is not here: for he is risen, as he said. Come, see the place where the Lord lay.

7 And go quickly, and tell his disciples that he has risen from the dead, and, behold, he goeth before you into Galilee, there shall ye see him: lo, I have told you.

8 And they departed quickly from the sepulcher with fear and great joy and did run to bring his disciples word.

Let us pray – Heavenly Father, I am Thy humble servant. I come today to speak of Your greatness, Your power, and Your love. Even for a man like me. You snatched me right out of the fire. And You gave me a whole new life and a new hope for eternity! Touch us all today Lord. As I give You control of this service.

In Jesus Mighty Name, Amen.

You may be seated.

Sermon August, 2021, I Shall Arise

Good day everyone! It's a great day to be in the house of the Lord. Amen! Thank you all for the cards and messages. My mom loved you all at Conarista Baptist very much!

It means a lot to my family and me.

(editor's note: Thank you Reynoldson Baptist, and Higher Ground Church IPHC, our friends, and the whole community for all your love and support during my mom's passing We love you very much!)

Normally when I give this message, it's dedicated to my dear friend Jeff Preziotti who helped lead me back to Christ. Of course, now it will mean so much more with my mother passing away. But, I wanted to come before you today to tell you a bit of my history. A bit of my testimony of the greatness of God! And the mercy of our Lord Jesus Christ. Also, the awesome power of His Holy Spirit. Amen.

I was adopted at nine months old from Lenoir, NC. My folks couldn't have kids, so they decided to adopt me. Praise the Lord. Interestingly enough, they said I was the most needy child in the room. But, God had a purpose and a plan for me as He does for us all. My biological father died in an automobile accident. So, my young mother decided to put me up for adoption. So you see, that's one reason I'm a strong advocate for children and family as a whole. What if my biological mother chose another path for me?

My new family also adopted a little girl. Her name is Vicki. She is my beloved sister! She's very dear to me. Especially now.

I remember one time looking at her when they adopted Vicki. We were very young, and they had us in the yard taking pictures. I said, "her head looks like a softball." lol

Mom and dad had, at one time, 13 horses, ducks, geese, bantam chickens, a dog, and all kinds of animals. We'd go to and ride in the horse shows and state fairs all over the east coast. Vicki and I talk about sleeping in the hay with the horses and bathing with the snakes. On one occasion, we were on a trail ride and had arrived at camp. We were getting our bath, and someone hollered, SNAKE! Yep, someone spotted a rattlesnake close by. That was exciting!

I Shall Arise

Growing up in a small farming community was a true blessing. We've had time recently to reflect and appreciate (Our Block) as we've come to call it. My grandmothers, on both sides, were women of great character and faith. They were very different people. But incredible women. I have no doubt that I'm alive and preaching the Gospel as a result of those two women's constant prayer. (of course, my mom and others as well)

Grandma Belle Byrum raised 9 children on a farm, predominantly alone, as her husband passed away when my father was small. Grandma Sally was a woman with a high school education but was one of the most intelligent people I've ever met! And they worked on a farm as well.

I got saved watching Billy Graham on television. I was about eight years old. Mr. Graham's TV shows were like the President's addresses back then. He came to all the stations! I remember it like it was last night! It was my time. The Lord spoke to me that night. He touched my little heart. When he gave that invitation, I asked The Lord Jesus to forgive my sins and come into my heart. It was a life-changing moment. And, of course, I couldn't see the bad things that lay just a few years down the road. All I knew was Mr. Graham told me the story of Jesus. How He loves me and wants me to go to be with Him in heaven when I die. I believed it then. I believe it now. God bless the ministry of Billy Graham. May it never cease or diminish until Jesus Christ rules from the earth!

I got a chance to stand at the 300-year podium in his little chapel in Asheville, NC. Our son Luther was going to school there. No one was there, really. We just went on a tour. I tell you, I knelt at the altar before stepping up to that podium! But I had to stand up there. I had to wrap my hands around its edges. I pleaded with God to help me be of any service to His Kingdom at all! And I praise God for all the great heroes of our faith! More importantly, the God of their faith that led them and protected them and their ministries! Glory to God!

I moved back to NC in 1997. I got a chance to study and work with our beloved Mr. Presley in Reynoldson Baptist. It was a powerful learning season for me. He actually asked me to fill in for him on a few occasions.

He never doubted me. I remember as a teenager, and our family unit was torn apart. Mr.P was right there. (Editor note: the example mentioned previously) John 3:16 A life lived out in public. When bad things come and seem to derail our hopes and dreams, we need a person of Christlike character to step in. Gently, but genuinely. When death comes, divorce, job layoffs, all those terrible things that hurt deeply! And your hopes and dreams seem to fade away before your very eyes. We need a strong person of Godly character to come wrap their arms around us. They don't even need to say a word! That's the man I'm trying to be today.

Mr. P put me in his pulpit when I felt unqualified as I was new to this thing called ministry. God used a few people to guide me along the way. I absorbed Bible lessons, human history, and the history of the church. Science and creative science studies. This was over many decades.

After many life events and changes, I found myself feeling again (unqualified). However, when men tell you that you're done because of a mistake or something has happened. That's not God's viewpoint! GOD SAYS GET UP!

> Proverbs 24:16-18
> 16 For a just man falleth seven times, and riseth up again: but the wicked shall fall into mischief.17 Rejoice not when thine enemy falleth, and let not thine heart be glad when he stumbleth: 18 Lest the Lord see it, and it displease him, and he turn away his wrath from him.

Ray Faircloth Sr. of Higher Ground church took me in a few years later. We had looked for a church for 2 years. As I had grown and God was calling me toward something more. I still had a lot of baggage and life scars to deal with. We all do. I remember meeting Pastor Ray Faircloth and shaking his hand. He said, "Hey how ya doing? I'm Ray."What's your background? I said, "I went to a Baptist church all my life. But I'm not focused on denominations at all." He said, I preach cover to cover right out of the Bible. I said great! Get up there, and let's see what ya got! I've been there ever since. It wasn't too long when God stirred my heart and soul again to preach. For the most part, God had taken music away on a larger scale. With all that was happening in the job market and the economy crashed.

God wanted me to focus directly on Him and His Word. God had to get the world out of me so through me, He could pull people out of the carnality of the world. I spoke to Pastor Ray about it. And he allowed me to step into his own pulpit. And he has never failed to allow me to stand IN HIS PULPIT to sing or preach when I've asked. Or when he asks me. In fact, he has several people who are capable of preaching or leading a church! That's a miracle and testimony to Godly character for a man to lead by example. God builds and creates. And everything should be in the order of the Kingdom of God. The best thing a man of God can do is train his successor! Pastor Ray has done that multiple times over! God used Pastor Ray and Higher Ground to allow me to grow in the POWER of the Holy Spirit. Which is lacking in the ministry today.

I enjoy the teachings of many heroes of the past, like William Branham, who had a remarkable healing ministry in the '30s-'60s. Smith Wigglesworth, also had an awesome healing ministry in Europe in the 1800s. Dr. Tony Evans is a current favorite. David Jeremiah is a scholar.

Lately, I've been greatly enjoying messages from the late Dr. Myles Monroe who was from the Bahamas. Dr. Monroe's life's work can be surmised on the teaching of the KINGDOM OF GOD! Incredible. That man realized his calling and his purpose early and leaped right on it!

One of my earliest messages was entitled – Why Gamble With Your Soul? I still preach it occasionally if led to. Studying the New Testament now sure brings a stark reality to what time we're living in. Wow! The hour is late, my friends! It's not time to be on the wrong side of the fence. Only eight people out of the whole planet got into Noah's ark! Now catch this, only one was raptured prior to the rain falling! That was Enoch.

Two scriptures were given to me two, and half years ago that stuck to me. Now I know why.

Revelation 1: 10-18
10 I was in the Spirit on the Lord's day and heard behind me a great voice, as of a trumpet,

11 Saying, I am Alpha and Omega, the first and the last: and, What thou seest, write in a book, and send it unto the seven churches which are in Asia, unto Ephesus, and unto Smyrna, and unto Pergamos, and unto Thyatira, and unto Sardis, and unto Philadelphia, and unto Laodicea.

12 And I turned to see the voice that spoke with me. And being turned, I saw seven golden candlesticks,

13 And in the midst of the seven candlesticks *one* like unto the Son of man, clothed with a garment down to the foot, and girt about the paps with a golden girdle.

14 His head and *his* hairs *were* white like wool, as white as snow, and his eyes *were* as a flame of fire,

15 And his feet like unto fine brass, as if they burned in a furnace, and his voice as the sound of many waters.

16 And he had in his right hand seven stars: and out of his mouth went a sharp two-edged sword: and his countenance *was* as the sun shineth in his strength.

17 And when I saw him, I fell at his feet as dead. And he laid his right hand upon me, saying unto me, Fear not, I am the first and the last:

18. I *am* he that liveth, and was dead, and, behold, I am alive forevermore, Amen, and have the keys of hell and of death.

19 Write the things which thou hast seen, and the things which are, and the things which shall be hereafter,

The second scripture is:

Romans 8:11
But if the Spirit of him that raised up Jesus from the dead dwell in you, he that raised up Christ from the dead shall also quicken your mortal bodies by his Spirit that dwelleth in you.

So if Hebrews 13:8 is true and states, He is the same yesterday, today, and forever, then we should awaken to the POWER THAT LIVES INSIDE OF US!

The God that lives in us! Amen!

Although I've been through many dangers, toils, and snares, I have already come. Glory to God! I press onward to the upward call in Christ Jesus! I am forgetting what's behind me and looking for hope in my future! Hallelujah! To live is Christ. To die is gain.

I will sing and preach the Good news of the Gospel of the Lord Jesus Christ. I will sing praises to my God! He's worthy! The bible says to go to the uttermost regions of the world and preach! Then the end will come. We must bear much fruit. That's the mandate and calling of every believer! We've been blessed and relaxed while the lost are perishing! God has shaken the ENTIRE PLANET OUT OF COMPLACENCY!

Did He get our undivided attention? We are to make straight the way for the soon-coming Kingdom of God! That's the whole purpose of life itself. It is to have God's Kingdom right here on earth where God is with us. We are to actually take part in God's administration here on earth.

Romans 13:11–14
11 And that, knowing the time, that now it is high time to awake out of sleep: for now is our salvation nearer than when we believed.

12 The night is far spent, the day is at hand: let us, therefore, cast off the works of darkness, and let us put on the armor of light.

13 Let us walk honestly, as in the day, not in rioting and drunkenness, not in chambering and wantonness, not in strife and envying.

14 But put ye on the Lord Jesus Christ, and make no provision for the flesh, to fulfill the lusts thereof.

1 Thessalonians 4:16-17
16 For the Lord himself shall descend from heaven with a shout, with the voice of the archangel, and with the trump of God: and the dead in Christ shall rise first:

17 Then we which are alive and remain shall be caught up together with them in the clouds, to meet the Lord in the air: and so shall we ever be with the Lord.

Let us stand in closing. As brother John and I spoke earlier, I'm going to come forward to pray with you if needed. The altar is open. As miss Becky calls it, the foot of the cross. In reality, we all need more of Jesus! God loves to hear from His children.

Let us pray – Lord, we need a touch from You today! We love You, Father! Please heal our wounded and sick. Mind, body, soul, and spirit. Father, I thank you for saving grace! Glory Hallelujah! For death could not hold You, Lord! You are alive and make us alive in You! Glory to God! May Your Spirit move in the hearts and souls of every lost one in our midst O God. Give us strength to endure and overcome! For no darkness can dwell where you are! Let Your light glow on the inside of all Your people. Wherever we go! To Your glory and praise, In Jesus Christ's Precious Name. Amen!

Blessing:
The Holy Spirit comes because Jesus Christ is indeed alive! I bless you in the Mighty Name of Jesus. Go in hope and power from God Almighty. To you and all your people, I bless you! Amen

Life Stories – When I Go to the Hospital, I Am Alive in Christ

No one wants to go to the hospital. None! Unfortunately, that's a requirement to keep our earth suit functioning. As I get older, I've had to succumb to the reality of going to the doctor. And even the hospital. I have had a few fairly challenging surgeries along the way. Some of which I partially induced due to over lifting in exercise and heavy labor. (Without adequate rest periods in between)

So it is with our life. We have a tendency to attempt to carry the load ourselves. This isn't the way God intended our lives to be.

Matthew 11:28–29
28 Come unto me, all ye that labor and are heavy laden, and I will give you rest.
29 Take my yoke upon you, and learn of me, for I am meek and lowly in heart: and ye shall find rest unto your souls.

Trust me when I tell you that the sooner we learn this from God, the better! It is not humanly possible to carry the burdens of this life all by ourselves. It doesn't matter your wealth, status, power, fame at all! You will not truly and fully be at peace without God. You and I do not have the capacity to overcome the assault of the enemy without the Holy Spirit. No one will achieve eternal rest without the Savior Jesus the Christ.

I remember in a time past when my sister Vicki had to be hospitalized with her lungs. I was in serious prayer! I literally got face down on the floor, crying out to God on her behalf. I really didn't get a response on how God was going to go with this. Ultimately, on the second day, I heard God say in my heart, "You go to her in the hospital and lay hands and pray for her." "You pray with your wife Eva and her husband, Danny." "You pray so the nurses can hear you."

What's important to know is He said to pray so the nurses could hear. So Eva and I went to the hospital. The nurses' station is located right outside her door. Danny's the only one there at the time. Danny said they had her sedated due to pain. I reached down and kissed her on the head. She was moaning. I said, Vicki, I'm here, and I'm going to pray for you. To everyone's surprise, she mouthed ok. Dany, Eva, and I prayed so the nurses could hear. Just as God said. Within a few days, Vicki was allowed to go to a step-down room. Within a few more days, she went home! Glory to God! Hallelujah!

I am very thankful and humbled by the fact we have a Father in heaven to pray to! Not every prayer is answered when or how we'd like. You see God's beyond time and space. I've seen many large and small miracles over the course of my life. That would make a wonderful reading! It's all about worship and faith. We can't have the faith required for miracles to happen without trusting in God and His Word. It's a trust issue.

Matthew 21:22 Jesus tells us to believe, and we will receive. This is speaking towards prayer in His will. (not a genie in a bottle)

The week my mom was in the hospital. I had a dream that God was going to take her home. It was one of those dreams you don't forget. Like it's happening right then. She had mentioned on the same day to her husband Jimmy that she didn't think she was going home from the hospital.

That afternoon, I went to see her before going to work. She had a tough day as they gave her kidney dialysis. It sure was hard to focus that night at work. Later that morning, when I got off, I returned to the hospital to check on my mom and pray.

I can't tell you how important my time with my mom was over those last two weeks. EVEN WHEN SHE WAS IN THE HOSPITAL! I tried to make her laugh about something. For a merry heart doeth a soul good! Amen.

As I passed through the doors, I was tired and concerned for sure. So, I stopped in the little hospital chapel to kneel down and pray. I knelt down

on the small altar. I first worshiped Almighty God, who alone is worthy of all our praise! And what came out next surprised me. I said, "Lord, if you're going to take my mamma home, please don't allow her to suffer here."
<u>And God heard my prayer and took my mamma home when I said amen.</u>

Psalms 116:15
15 Precious in the sight of the LORD is the death of his saints.

My mamma was carried by the strong arms of God's heavenly angels straight into the arms of King Jesus! And I tell you this, I plan to go there too! Just believe it! And receive it…

Ephesians 2:1–7
We were once lost. Dead spiritually in our sins. But, Jesus has now quickened us! Amen! He has made us alive! He found us and washed us up. And set us free! Praise God!

1 And you hath he quickened, who were dead in trespasses and sins,

2 Wherein in time past ye walked according to the course of this world, according to the prince of the power of the air, the spirit that now worketh in the children of disobedience:

3 Among whom also we all had our conversation in times past in the lusts of our flesh, fulfilling the desires of the flesh and of the mind, and were by nature the children of wrath, even as others.

4 But God, who is rich in mercy, for his great love wherewith he loved us,

5 Even when we were dead in sins, hath quickened us together with Christ, (by grace ye are saved,)

6 And hath raised us up together, and made us sit together in heavenly places in Christ Jesus:

7 That in the ages to come, he might shew the exceeding riches of his grace in his kindness toward us through Christ Jesus.

I BLESS YOU ALL. JESUS IS ALIVE!
NOW SO ARE WE!
Go in peace, and the love with all joy abounding always!
Amen

CHAPTER 6

New Kingdom

Scripture

~~~~

Revelation Chapter 21

1 And I saw a new heaven and a new earth: for the first heaven and the first earth were passed away, and there was no more sea.

2 And I John saw the holy city, new Jerusalem, coming down from God out of heaven, prepared as a bride adorned for her husband.

3 And I heard a great voice out of heaven saying, Behold, the tabernacle of God *is* with men, and he will dwell with them, and they shall be his people, and God himself shall be with them, *and be* their God.

4 And God shall wipe away all tears from their eyes, and there shall be no more death, neither sorrow, nor crying, neither shall there be any more pain: for the former things are passed away.

5 And he that sat upon the throne said, Behold, I make all things new. And he said unto me, Write: for these words are true and faithful.

6 And he said unto me, It is done. I am Alpha and Omega, the beginning and the end. I will give unto him that is athirst of the fountain of the water of life freely.

7 He that overcometh shall inherit all things, and I will be his God, and he shall be my son.

8 But the fearful, and unbelieving, and the abominable, and murderers, and whoremongers, and sorcerers, and idolaters, and all liars, shall have their part in the lake which burneth with fire and brimstone: which is the second death.

9 And there came unto me one of the seven angels which had the seven vials full of the seven last plagues, and talked with me, saying, Come hither, I will shew thee the bride, the Lamb's wife.

10 And he carried me away in the spirit to a great and high mountain, and shewed me that great city, the holy Jerusalem, descending out of heaven from God,

11 Having the glory of God: and her light *was* like unto a stone most precious, even like a jasper stone, clear as crystal,

12 And had a wall great and high, *and* had twelve gates, and at the gates, twelve angels, and names written thereon, which are *the names* of the twelve tribes of the children of Israel:

13 On the east three gates, on the north three gates, on the south three gates, and on the west three gates.

14 And the wall of the city had twelve foundations, and in them the names of the twelve apostles of the Lamb.

15 And he that talked with me had a golden reed to measure the city, and the gates thereof, and the wall thereof.

16 And the city lieth foursquare, and the length is as large as the breadth: and he measured the city with the reed, twelve thousand furlongs. The length and the breadth and the height of it are equal.

17 And he measured the wall thereof, an hundred *and* forty *and* four cubits, *according to* the measure of a man, that is, of the angel.

18 And the building of the wall of it was *of* jasper: and the city *was* pure gold, like unto clear glass.

19 And the foundations of the wall of the city *were* garnished with all manner of precious stones. The first foundation *was* jasper, the second, sapphire, the third, a chalcedony, the fourth, an emerald,

20 The fifth, sardonyx, the sixth, sardius, the seventh, chrysolite, the eighth, beryl, the ninth, a topaz, the tenth, a chrysoprase, the eleventh, a jacinth, the twelfth, an amethyst.

21 And the twelve gates *were* twelve pearls, every several gates was of one pearl: and the street of the city *was* pure gold as if it were transparent glass.

22 And I saw no temple therein: for the Lord God Almighty, and the Lamb are the temple of it.

23 And the city had no need of the sun, neither of the moon, to shine in it: for the glory of God did lighten it, and the Lamb *is* the light thereof.

24 And the nations of them which are saved shall walk in the light of it: and the kings of the earth do bring their glory and honor into it.

25 And the gates of it shall not be shut at all by day: for there shall be no night there.

26 And they shall bring the glory and honor of the nations into it.

27 And there shall in no wise enter into it anything that defileth, neither *whatsoever* worketh abomination, nor *maketh* a lie: but they which are written in the Lamb's book of life.

Sermon – Why Gamble with Your Soul?

Original date: 9/6/15

Hebrews 11:1 Faith is being sure of what you hope for.
> Our hope must be in The Lord Jesus Christ for our salvation.
> (for the forgiveness of our sin)
> <u>Why would we gamble with our souls? 9-6-15</u>
> First, let's discuss what makes up a person.
> A person is made up of 3 parts. Body, soul, and spirit.

1. The body is what I call our earth suit. (what we live in)

   Genesis 1:2-6
   And the Lord formed man of the dust of the earth and breathed into his nostrils – The Breath of Life.

The difference between people and animals is we are made in God's image.

   Genesis 2:26
   and God said, "Let Us make man in our image after our likeness and let them have dominion over all the fish of the sea and over the fowl of the air and over the cattle and over ALL the earth and over every creepeth thing that creepeth upon the earth."

Note: what God calls alive is alive and what God calls dead is dead. What has the breath of God is alive.

2. The spirit is of dealing with the mind and mental characteristics of a man.

His conscientiousness, reasoning, and thought are all parts of the spirit of man.

Websters' definition of the spirit is: having awareness or knowledge. A man has the totality of mortal states and possesses perceptions and feelings as well as thoughts in the widest sense.

> Proverbs 20:27
> The spirit of a man is the candle of The Lord, searching all the inward parts of the belly.

There used to be an old saying that the easiest way to a man's heart is through his stomach. AMEN LOL (I relate to that)

> John 4:24
> God is Spirit. We are to worship Him in spirit and truth.

NOTE: Genesis 6:3 God's Spirit will not strive with man forever.

2. Soul – The soul is the real you! It's the eternal part of mankind. It's the part of you that lives forever. Matthew 10:28 – says not to fear man, but fear the One who's able to destroy both the body and the soul in hell.

Jesus said in Matthew 22:37 – "You shall love the Lord your God w/ all your heart, with all your soul, and with all your mind. This is the first and great commandment." This covers the mind, body, soul, and spirit.

Now, if we have clarified that God is A Spiritual Eternal Being and throughout all the Old Testament scriptures, God Himself said – "I AM THAT I AM." And in the New Testament, Jesus said in Revelation," I AM THE FIRST AND THE LAST THE BEGINNING AND THE END." He who created us in HIS image being eternal, we must be an eternal being as well, correct?

So let us reason together. Where is the breakdown?

It boils down to this fact, a person falls into two different groups. Saved and Not saved.

1. Saved – A person who accepts Jesus Christ as Lord and Savior. They believe that Jesus died for the forgiveness of their sins and are BORN AGAIN.

It runs all the way from Adam the first man to us. We ALL are born into sin from the fall of Adam and Eve, the first man and woman.

Like Abraham, the great man in the Old Testament, it was accounted to him as faith because he believed. Likewise, in the New Testament in Revelations, we are saved by faith.

2. Unsaved – An unsaved person is one who doesn't believe in Jesus and His death on the cross for eternal salvation. They actually forfeit their place in The Kingdom of God.

It doesn't mean they are necessarily a bad person; they simply don't believe.

A person who is saved believes what John 3:16-18 says – God so loved the world that He gave His one and only Son, that ANY who believes in Him shall be saved. For God sent not His Son to condemn the world, but through His Son, they might be saved. He that believes in Him is not condemned. But who doesn't believe is condemned already.

Because he has not believed in the only begotten Son of God (Jesus), the name above all names.

This, my friends, is, in fact, the only unforgivable sin. As it's against the Holy Spirit who is calling to all our hearts to come to Jesus for salvation and hope.

Our own brother Casey at Higher Ground church said, "you know enough already to be saved."

Friends, I must say -no decision at all is a (NO) to the calling of Jesus to salvation.

<u>WE MUST CHOOSE OUR DESTINATION</u>

Heaven – Is also known as paradise wherever God is. It's where His throne is.

Ecclesiastes 5:2, Isaiah 66:1, and Psalm 145:1

The Kingdom of God is an eternal kingdom.

Luke 23:43 – Jesus told the thief on the cross who asked Him to remember him (when He comes into His Kingdom), that this day you'll be with me in paradise. Amen!

Revelation 21:1 speaks of a new heaven and new earth as the old heaven and earth will pass away.

Jesus said – "behold, I make all things new!"

In heaven, there are no more tears or suffering OF ANY KIND! It's a place of joy unimaginable. The eye can't even see all the colors available to us here on earth. Imagine what we'll be able to see, touch, and taste there, where all things are perfect. Including us…

Heaven is a place of reunion of lost loved ones that were saved. It's a place where there is no time to hinder us. There's no end to life at its absolute full potential.

There is NO DEATH, SICKNESS, SORROW, OR HURT OF ANY KIND! For the wages of sin is death. And death can't enter there… A SUPER AMEN TO THAT.

Hell –
Revelation 21:8 But the cowardly, unbelieving, abominable, murders, sexually immoral, sorcerer, idolaters, and all liars will have their place in the lake of fire and brimstone, which is the second death. Hell was never designed for any human being. It was built for Satan and the fallen angels after they attempted to overthrow God in a war in heaven.

This place is currently located in the center of the earth. It will eventually be thrown in its entirety into the lake of fire in a final judgment by The Lord Jesus Christ.

Luke 16:24 – The rich man who had died and gone to hell said, "I'm tormented in this flame!" So we see hell is a place of lasting torment.

One of the best descriptions of hell I've found in modern times is Bill Wiese's 23 minutes in hell. He had what the apostle Paul calls a vision of hell. And he gives a very intense description of what hell's like. He also uses MANY scriptures as reference points.

Bill also clearly states that it's not his wish that people believe his vision. But more importantly, people make a decision to not go there! Christ clearly spoke much more of hell than he did of heaven. Why He doesn't want ANY OF US TO GO THERE!

However, without a savior, that's where we'll go.

King David of Israel said – "I see the wonders of your fingers and what is man that you are mindful of him.

Romans 1:20 Since the creation of the world and His invisible attributes, His eternal power, and divine nature have been clearly seen being understood through what has been made, so they are without excuse.

Not only is Jesus mindful of you and me, He loves you and me in a way that can not compare with anyone on this planet. It is called agape love. It's a perfect, pure love in the most powerful sense. Much stronger than even an earthly mother or father could feel.

It's a love that bought back humanity from the clutches of satan by God Himself, taking our place on that old rugged cross. Jesus put Himself on that cross to defeat death, hell, and the grave. He was God in human flesh on that cross.

Because of what sin did through Adam to destroy our fellowship with an Eternal God, Jesus restored it by breaking every chain Satan put on mankind. GLORY TO GOD!

And when it was over-Jesus said, "IT IS FINISHED, FATHER INTO THY HANDS I COMMIT MY SPIRIT!"

Let us stand.

The question is, where do you and I commit our spirit and our soul?

Joshua said, "choose you this day whom you'll serve." Not tomorrow or the next day – BUT DO IT TODAY! And keep choosing daily to serve Him.

Time is of essence, my friends. You're not too old or too young, and if you're breathing, it's not too late to choose Him. It's simple – just say

JESUS SAVE ME. Forgive me. That's it. But say it from the heart. Jesus, save me. I believe You died on that cross and rose to life for me!

Heal me! And fill me with Your Holy Spirit. Change my whole life! In Jesus Christ's Name, Amen!

You folks that are saved – dig deeper in your faith. Get closer to Him than ever before.

Trust Him with all your heart and soul! Glory to God!

And be bold in your faith and love for folks. The fields are ripe for harvest, but the workers are few. We need to all draw closer as we see the time's drawing near for our meeting with the Lord Jesus Christ. The King of Glory. I bless you all! Go in peace and power of God Almighty!

God bless you all, and let us unite in prayer for one another and people all over the world.

Amen

Ricky Byrum

Life Stories – On My Way Home

In all my years traveling with the horses and then later in music, I always looked forward to seeing new places. Granted, being in bands that concentrated on original music, we didn't get to be full-on road warriors. But the fact remains, I've moved around some. Getting to my destination wasn't as fun as arriving by no means. Much like when one plans a vacation, getting there and back is very tiring. So it is in this journey we call life. How little we stop to smell the roses along the way. Then, one day it dawned on us; we practically missed the whole ride!

Dr. Myles Monroe stated in one of his messages that when he was young, he made it a point to make good memories. It takes away Satan's number one target, the human mind. That's very, very true! Are we making – good memories?

One of the joys of going to different places is enjoying the food! (of course)

Another is seeing the change in culture, music, designs, and structures.

Eva and I experienced some of this when we first got married. It was a bit harder to get away for a while as we're a big, blended family! A trip to any fast-food chain is a costly event for us!

However, we did get out not too long ago (just prior to the Pandemic) to Edenton, NC. In 2021 we escaped to the Outer Banks and even a short stay on some lakes in Suffolk, Va. I really enjoyed that! It was nice to shut down for a minute. Most people typically don't get that enough, in my opinion.

Have you ever noticed that one of the best parts of getting away is coming home?

It's a rare occasion to go somewhere that you just don't want to leave. Wherever I go, I try to see what it's like for those that live there. But it's usually such a wonderful feeling getting home, unpacked, and resting.

I'm sure that's why most people like to remember a better or more simple time in their lives. Whether it was fewer responsibilities or because they were younger etc.

My early childhood is overflowing with great memories of playing sports, riding horses, dirt bikes, and dirt clog wars! We rode bicycles all over this side of the county. I was fourteen riding a bike with Larry, the first time I saw Eva. She was getting a drink out of a vending machine. WOW! Larry told me to quit staring at her as her mamma was in the car. You're going to get in trouble! I told him I can't help it! Well, we're married now. I guess it's ok to confess it. Amen?

Music was off the chain! It didn't matter what music you liked; it was awesome! And the musicians actually played and sang those parts. We had family reunions where the FOOD WAS OUT OF THIS WORLD! That's why church functions need to return to par to bring back some of this home cooking!

My life's journey has been a long road. Yet, It's gone by so fast. I appreciate every kind word ever spoken over me. I ask everyone that I ever hurt to forgive me if I've caused you any pain. As I certainly forgive you!

I thank My Precious Lord for all the people, places, and opportunities He's so gloriously given me. It's been one amazing ride! My hope is that God will take my little offerings and manifest them into something magnificent! May He use the works of my hands to bring Him glory and blessings to others. Globally! And most importantly, draw others unto the Lord Jesus Christ! That people will be saved, filled with the Holy Ghost, devils cast out and tread upon! A work where people's lives are wondrously changed forever. Amen!

My life's goal now has been streamlined and simplified.

I WANT TO FINISH WELL!

I want to make my Father in Heaven proud of me.

It's a feeling that guides me each day. It affects the choices I make and steers my path. You see, if I am pleasing Him by what I'm doing (as it's in His will), everything else falls into place. My everyday tasks, including caring for my family, will be done well. As He loves us all unequivocally.

This world isn't my home yet. It will be one day after The Lord brings it back to a perfect state. In the meantime, I'm doing my best to please my Father.

You see, I'm on my journey home. The apostle Paul said, to live is Christ. To die is gain. Philippians 1:21. It's a longing I've had my whole life. I just couldn't explain it or comprehend it. Don't get me wrong, I still enjoy the beauty of God's creation we call earth. It's so wonderful! But, I can only imagine what it will be like when He returns it to its original state of Eden! Amen.

But so are you! We all are headed to an eternal destination.

2 Timothy 1:9
Who hath saved us, and called us with a holy calling, not according to our works, but according to his own purpose and grace, which was given us in Christ Jesus before the world began,

Luke 12:32
Fear not, little flock, for it is your Father's good pleasure to give you the kingdom.

John 14:3
And if I go and prepare a place for you, I will come again, and receive you unto myself, that where I am, there ye may also be.

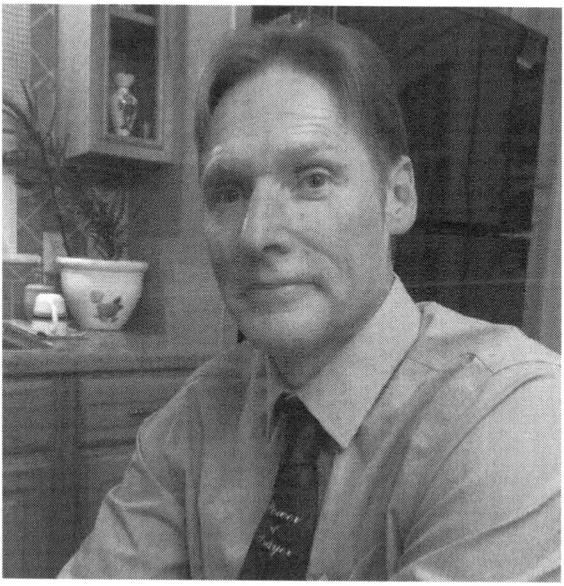

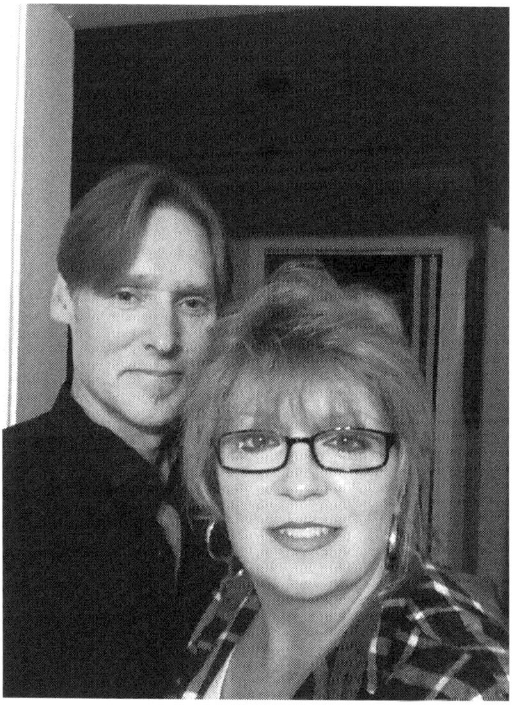

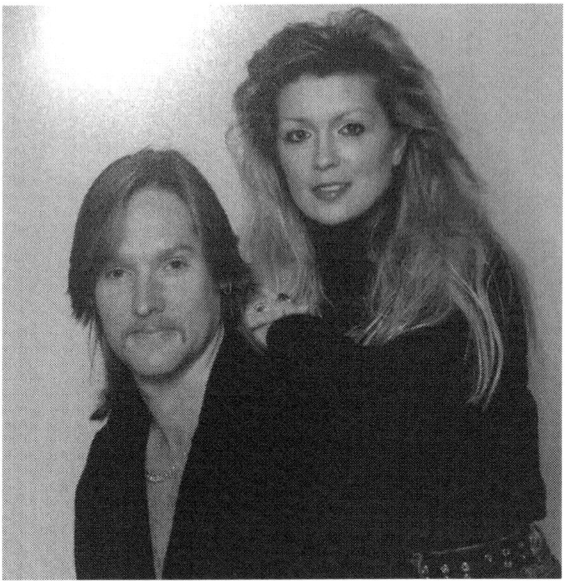

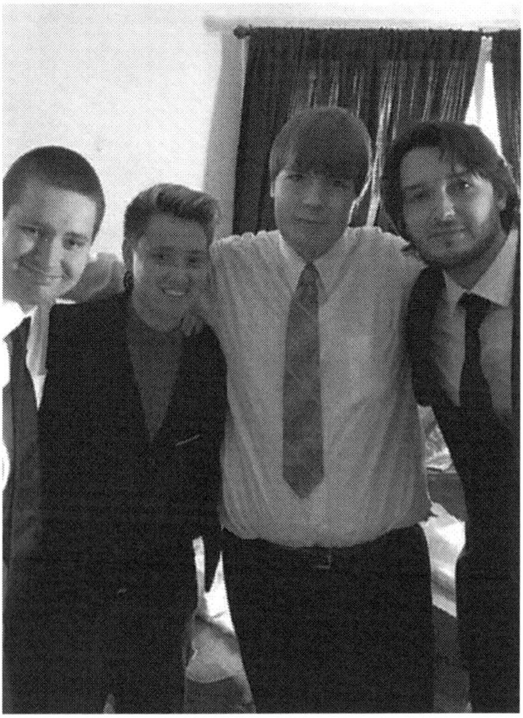

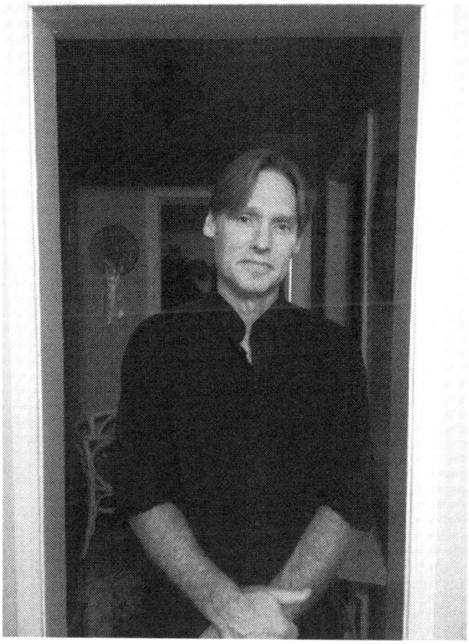

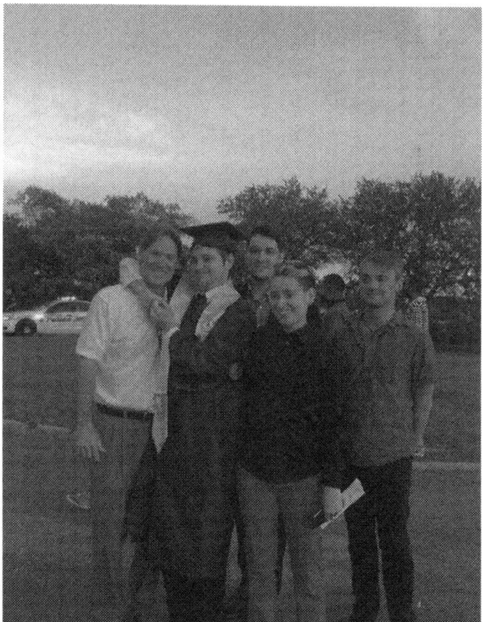

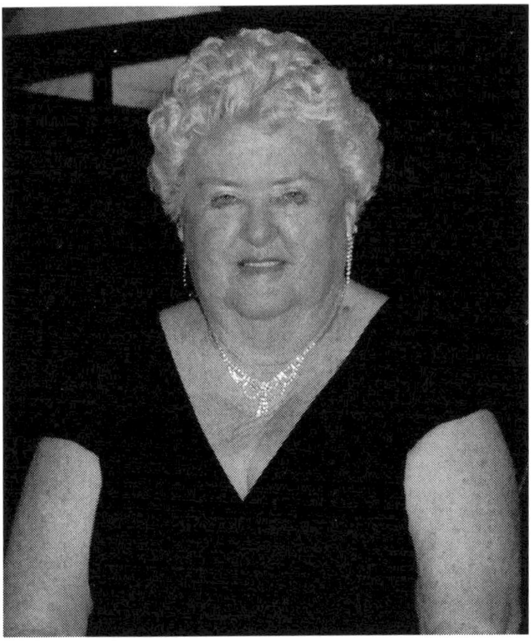

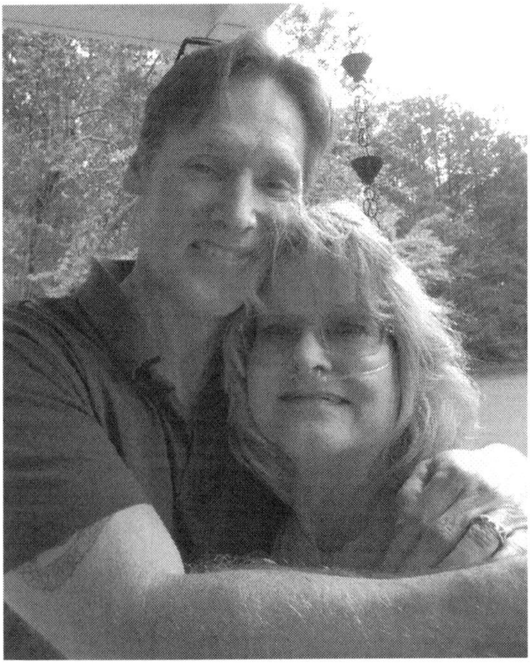

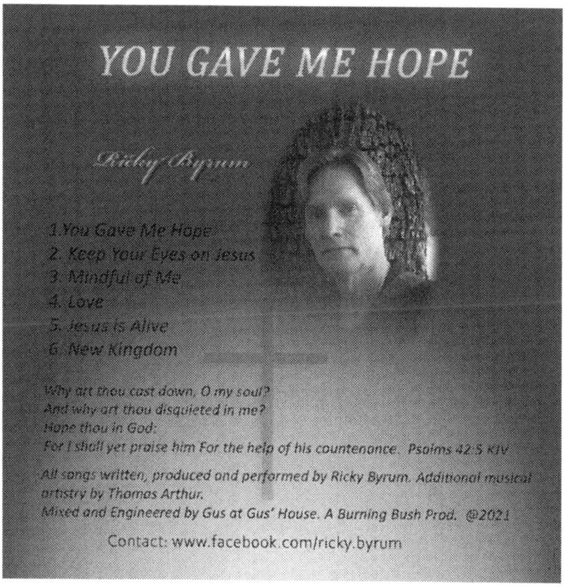
YOU GAVE ME HOPE
Ricky Byrum
1.You Gave Me Hope
2. Keep Your Eyes on Jesus
3. Mindful of Me
4. Love
5. Jesus is Alive
6. New Kingdom
Why art thou cast down, O my soul?
And why art thou disquieted in me?
Hope thou in God:
For I shall yet praise him For the help of his countenance. Psalms 42:5 KJV
All songs written, produced and performed by Ricky Byrum. Additional musical artistry by Thomas Arthur.
Mixed and Engineered by Gus at Gus' House. A Burning Bush Prod. @2021
Contact: www.facebook.com/ricky.byrum

Postscript

So, as we come to the end of this little book,

You Gave Me Hope (My Story)

It's really His story. His hand was guiding me. From a scraggly head little boy. To a long-haired teenager. Now, I'm a middle-aged man.

He was walking with me holding my hand. (On my journey home). Home, a new Kingdom not made by human hands.

The reality is, He's preparing you and me, in the here and now, to become an intricate part of the Kingdom process. And although it seems long, it's all set to His timing and planning.

Psalm 42:11
11 Why art thou cast down, O my soul? And why art thou disquieted within me? Hope thou in God: for I shall yet praise him, who is the health of my countenance, and my God.

Romans 15:13
"Now the God of hope fill you with all joy and peace in believing, that ye may abound in hope, through the power of the Holy Ghost."

Your brother in Christ, Ricky Byrum
3/8/22

Made in the USA
Middletown, DE
12 September 2022